HIS NAME
AND HIS RING

DONALD ALLEN

ISBN: 978-1-962402-45-3 (hardcover)
978-1-962402-44-6 (paperback)

(The Message Bible has been used in many of the scriptural quotes in this book, but the author also double checked in King James. If a quote is not specifically identified, it is likely from the Message Bible.)

Please send comments and requests to the author:
jonahjoe2025@gmail.com

Published by

Fideli Publishing, Inc.
119 W. Morgan St.
Martinsville, IN 46151
www.FideliPublishing.com

HIS NAME
AND HIS RING

INTRODUCTION

Do you understand your salvation in Christ? What if it is something more than you have understood? What if you're stuck in a spiritual wilderness because you've never really understood?

Most of us are familiar with the tried-and-true method of Roman's Road. Such as, "For all have sinned and fallen short of the glory of God." But what I'm offering comes in from an entirely different angle with a rather different vision. Perhaps a better understanding. A very powerful understanding.

When an altar call is being given or a witnessing encounter is in progress, what is really happening? And it is something that everyone on planet earth understands.

Jesus is asking, "Will you marry Me?"

Can a mortal marry God? Would God really offer such a thing? And what does it mean that He is? Especially, if you've said, "Yes." Will God put His Ring on my finger?

What does it all mean?

CHAPTER ONE

*"*__*Because*__ *he has set his love upon me, there-*
fore I will deliver him; I will set him on high,
__*because*__ *he has known my name."*

— Psalms 91:14 KJV

What is salvation in Christ? It is a spiritual marriage. Does the average person understand this? Can a man marry God? And yet, is not the biblical description of marriage understood by most people and gives a much closer understanding of what the saved relationship is? Can we prove this? I believe we can, and easily so.

God's Word to us, the Bible, is all about a courtship and marriage from beginning to end. It begins with God creating Adam, but He creates him alone and lonely. As Adam realizes his loneliness, God creates Eve, and we have the first God ordained marriage when God declared them to be one. This all happens in the first few chapters of God's Word to us. These are the very opening scenes of the biblical journey ahead.

Go to the end of God's Word to us, the Book of Revelation, and what do we see? The wedding Feast of the Lamb! God's Church as the Bride! A great wedding in Heaven! From beginning to end and all through the middle we see a spiritual courtship and eventual marriage between God, (in the form of God the Son), and mankind. The wedding in heaven appears to be the journey destination.

Jesus comes in like a Knight in shining armor to rescue His damsel in distress from a great dragon. It's all there, and it's all true. It's the ultimate hero's journey of love and danger. Our hero does not fail in His fight against evil, and now a door is opened for the damsel to choose life with her Knight forever, or not. So, the question becomes, just how does one become part of this incredible supernatural Bride? And make no mistake, she is very supernatural.

If we're "going-forward" to an altar call so Jesus can save us from our sins and a place called hell. Do we understand how He does that? We're told we must be born-again. Okay, I kind of get that. So, we acknowledge we are a sinner, ask to be saved, we repeat a prayer after someone, almost like a formula, and hopefully the person is sincere and they are saved. But do they understand they just entered a spiritual marriage to Christ? They now have a person they are One with to consider in all things. A person they love. *"Because he has set his love upon me..."*

Have we fallen in love with the person and vision of our Lord? Or have we been a mail-order bride, not the real thing? Are we in love? Or feeling forced? Are we living a romance, or some kind of manipulation? Do we see the romance? Or is this a new idea for you?

In other words, the next day when we wake up, there is someone else in that bed with us. And more than in the bed, He's actually in us! By way of the Holy Spirit. We have entered a married relationship with God, built on love, not fear, and He is our head because we are the female (symbolically) in this marriage. Even as He is head of the Church, which we are now a part of, which is the Bride of the Lamb. We are that Bride! We are now ONE.

I believe our understanding would be so much greater if we knew Jesus is calling us to a spiritual marriage. That would likely prevent some false salvations from ever happening, and so much better prepare the new convert for what is expected of them. But how would we go about doing it? How could you personally use this method for witnessing if you wanted to?

Probably most of you, if you know your Bible very well, already realize how easy it would be to use this approach. I think the best way to know how to use it is actually by considering what the Bible says about marriage, and how it affects our relationship to someone.

Marriage also carries "Legal" rights. Very important legal rights! This is the way God chose to save us! A way speaking of love and relationship, not a way of condemnation and law. We feel condemnation before salvation, as we should, condemnation leading to true repentance. But not after, because we are forgiven and birthed into His Name! Is it a marriage or a birth? It seems to be both! *I will set him on high "because" he has known my Name. WOW!*

We need His name! Everyone needs His name! The beauty and wisdom of what God has done is worth writing a book about, and that is exactly what I am attempting to do. Let it go forth like a godly sword against our dark enemy and the curse of ignorance. Be this book small or large when done, is up to God. I have many thoughts on this subject I hope to share.

Such as, why did the man who was blessed with incredible wisdom from God only write three books in the Bible? And how does that relate to our subject? You will see. Only Solomon could write three books, like stair steps, and then you can go no higher. In his wisdom he knew the third book said it all and there was no higher place to go. And yet, that book has been questioned by many people if it should even be in the Bible! This shows a complete lack of understanding. David understood and lived, what his son would later write.

This book might be for men more than women, because as men, we're not use to being in the position of the Bride. It's more difficult for us to wrap our macho brains around this. But let me mention this one thing, for starters. What happens when the Bride is officially married to the Groom? (And I'm not talking about the bedroom, guys. Shame on us. LOL)

If you haven't figured it out, here's the answer: She takes on the Grooms last name! And a ring is put on her finger! What happens then? *What is yours becomes hers! What is yours just became hers also!* That's how God saved us! When I entered marriage with Jesus, I got His Name! And what is His became mine! His perfection, His holiness, His righteousness, His Kingdom, His warrior angels, His promises, His spiritual armor of light, the mind of Christ, His peace, joy, love, *everything*! Including His entrance into Heaven because heaven now belongs to me too! Wow! He set me on high! It even says we are seated at the right hand of Christ! *We need His name!*

Everyone needs His name! (I do not apologize for so many exclamation marks on this point. It deserves even more!)

> *"I will set him on high*
> **because** *he has known my Name."*

People are dying every day. Some suddenly, with no chance to change. People go to a concert and out of nowhere, a person with a death wish starts shooting people and many suddenly die. A car accident and suddenly dead. A fire in the house and you never woke up. *Everyone needs His name!* And they need it now! Not later, when they might get around to it.

God is chasing us, calling to us, asking, *will you marry me?* Do you love me more than darkness? Will you stop running away, turn around, and say "Yes" to my proposal? You see, a marriage based on love requires a "yes" from the female. A forced marriage, or arranged marriage, is not based on love. Salvation is a marriage based on love, based on a "yes" from the female. The male is asking, but will she say "yes"? God is not looking for a forced marriage. Neither does He need to.

Heaven is a place of perfection; there is no sin there. I'm not perfect, but I'm engaged to the One who is, and by Jewish tradition, engagement is almost like already married. Or perhaps our salvation is like two people who love each other so much, but they are too poor to have a big wedding, so they go to a justice of the peace, and they promise each other they will have a big wedding in a Church as soon as they can. And the wedding at the end of this journey sounds pretty mind blowing!

So, I show up at the pearly gates. A guardian angel looks at me and says, you are unworthy of entrance. You may not enter! I tell them my name. They don't believe me. I bring up my hand revealing my wedding Ring and say, "Take a good look at the Rock on this finger." (Jesus is the Rock of my salvation.) The angel's eyes quickly enlarge, he suddenly bows and says, "Please forgive me, enter into the glorious home belonging to you and your great Husband."

"I am sorry for my haste, Sir, Mam. The Bride of the Lamb is always welcome in the home that belongs to her. I will not make this mistake again."

I then freely enter into *my* home, *my* city, *my* eternity. It's *mine*, and I belong there. *My Husband and I possess it together.* But there must be love. Jesus gave two commands, and they both require the God kind of love. Jesus fulfilled the law in love.

Only one person came to this earth with the audacity claiming to be God, to be without sin, and would rise from the dead. I'd say pretty good proof if you can do it. History books tell of the day they nailed Him to that cross. The Apostles scattered when they saw Him die. What good is a dead man? It was over. Peter even went back to fishing. (And Peter loved fishing.)

What could have happened that caused those men to later give their lives completely, even unto death, the history books record. But that Jesus proved Himself alive to them, risen from the dead! And many other witnesses also testified of such at that time. And if so, out of all the religions, He is the only one who has ever accomplished such a thing! And we can marry Him???

So, whose name do you want? Do you want Mohamad? Some New Age guru? Buddha? And how do you propose to get their name? Can you marry a dead man? I think it would be a pretty lifeless and boring relationship. Pun intended.

Therefore, there is only one way to Heaven. That way is the person of Jesus Christ! He is our Knight in shining armor who accepted the mission from God our Father. And God set up a marriage. We *need* His *name*. It is the place for the Bride of the Lamb, and none other. You got to have the right Ring on your finger if you hope to be there. *The Ring higher than them all!*

In the second movie of "Dunes", the young hero gains the ability to see all possible futures. And out of those futures he sees ONE path to their victory. Only ONE. And it is the path they must take if they are not going to die.

In the Marvel Movie, End Games, Doctor Strange searches all the possible futures, millions of them, and in the end, he says, there is only One path in all the millions in which we might win. There is no saving your soul from hell without possessing His name, and that happens by a spiritual marriage that happens when you're born-again in Christ. One path. One Ring. ***One Ring that overcomes them all.***

There is so much, so much, so much more to be said on this subject, including the dimension the book of Hosea adds to all this. The Song of Songs and book of Hosea have much to say about this. And in truth, every book in your Bible has so much to say about this, and we have just begun.

CHAPTER TWO

If you have a marriage that has survived for any time, you know, as wonderful as it can be, marriage is also work. If our two lovers are going to be happy in their relationship there will be personal changes that must happen. It's not just you anymore. It's you and her. Or you and him. And you will work out those changes because you love that person, not because you fear them. A marriage of fear is not good. Fear is not love.

If children come into the picture, which happens most of the time, now you both have the concern of how to work together to protect, provide, and love your children. The same is true in this spiritual marriage to Christ. As you grow in Christ and begin leading others to Him, they begin looking up to you as an example of being married to Christ. You become a spiritual mother and father to them. If you suddenly veer away from faithfulness to the marriage, what affect does that have on the children you have brought into God's Kingdom?

Salvation is not just a prayer at an altar, it is a marriage to God! He greatly loves us and only wants to see us prosper in His Spirit. But if we are sabotaging the relationship, bad things will eventually come. He is waiting for us to do the work honoring the marriage. If we are true in our love and vows, the marriage will be blessed.

The Bible is absolutely a love story. It is the greatest Romance book from cover to cover. It is the incredible event of a Knight saving a damsel in destress from a great dragon. We are the damsel in destress. A person who does not see this will likely not believe they need to get saved.

"Saved from what?"

"There is a dragon!"

"Where? I don't see one. You just got a vivid imagination, sir."

"But, sir, death is the dragon, and we all end up in its clutches! Please reconsider your lack of wisdom! Everyone dies! This is not imagination! This is reality! Wake up!"

In any adventure involving possible mortality, there is danger and things to be feared. We are not controlled by these fears, but true wisdom enables us to use fear to our advantage and find the "one good path". There is a God to be feared if we refuse to acknowledge Him as God and heed His perfect advice. And there is a dragon, whom we cannot defeat with mortal weapons. We cannot defeat him at all. Only God can and already has. We enter that victory through the spiritual marriage into His Name. We do not win because of our strength against the enemy. We win because of our love for God / Jesus.

Women may not like this, but God's word says women are the weaker vessel. Women have beauty, which is a powerful thing, but the man has more strength, therefore the man does the heavy lifting. But we, as born-again men need to learn how to let God do the heavy lifting!

Simple faith, prayer, and love can affect more things than our trying to force things. We need faith more than force. Let go and let God do the heavy lifting. Jesus offers us peace and rest. This is faith. It is a blessing of our marriage.

> "But I want you to know that the head of every man is Christ, the head of woman is man, and the head of Christ is God." — 1st Corinthians 11:3

> "Husbands, likewise, dwell with them with understanding, giving honor to the wife, as to the weaker vessel, and as being heirs together of the grace of life, that your prayers may not be hindered." — 1st Peter 3:7 (NKJ)

We think force is the way of God for us, as men. It's really the opposite. We frustrate God's supernatural working through us by trying to exert our own force and bring about some imagined goal. The Children of Israel, desiring meat in the wilderness, reveals to us a way of focusing on what God brings into the camp, not what we spend day and night running after. Unless the Lord builds the house, the laborers labor in vain. God gives His beloved sleep! Rest! Faith! Even the supernatural. He does the heavy lifting. As men, we got to get a grip on this.

Fear has its purpose when properly facilitated, but make no mistake, our marriage to Christ is based on love. Fear may open our eyes to who He is, but once we see Him, there should be wisdom and love. Once we are married, only if we play the spiritual harlot should fear enter anymore. And love is stronger than will power. A life of love will get you farther than relying on your own will power alone. Love and faith.

> *"But for right now, until that completeness, we have three things to do to lead us toward that consummation: Trust steadily in God, hope unswervingly, love extravagantly. And the best of the three is love."*
>
> — 1st Corinthians 13:13 (Message)

Some people will wake up in bed the next day after getting saved and not think anything about it. They might think, "Well, I guess I'm saved now, but I still got to get to work and pay the bills. And I guess I go to Church on Sundays now."

Others will wake up and say, "Oh my God, I married God yesterday! Now what? Maybe I better at least talk to Him a little bit before I rush off to work. I can't wait for the next get-together with my new family. And look at this Ring on my finger! I got to show this off!" (See the difference?)

These are two very different understandings of what they did yesterday at something called Church. Marriage to Christ has so much to offer in the supernatural that you do not understand yet. The one individual will be led to those treasures in the Spirit and experience a relationship in Christ more powerful than any other you can ever have. The other person will likely wonder in the wilderness for many years and constantly wonder if God is real. God was greatly feared in the wilderness, especially at Mount Sinia/Horeb. It's more of a fear relationship.

One will be enjoying God's supernatural promised land, the other a dry desert of struggles and stress. And if you think I'm talking about money here, you're wrong. In God's supernatural land, money means little. It's faith that counts. Righteous faith is the powerhouse in God's Kingdom, and it works in very peaceful ways. If something is needed, and it's "in the camp" of God's will (to be explained later), the money will be there. You cannot serve God and money. Jesus made that plain.

It's a whole different way of living, walking by faith and not by sight, living in the Spirit and not the flesh. God's Kingdom is a Sky Kingdom (to also be explained later). Jesus said to consider the birds. But Jesus will always provide for His wife and His house. He is the greatest provider and protector.

The Promised Land was a place flowing with milk and honey, but if we're still in the wilderness, then we're not experiencing that, and that's our fault, not His. He desires to lead us there. The man leads. The Lord is my Shepherd. If we're wise, we learn to follow. But He will be with us even in the wilderness. He will not leave or forsake us.

In a marriage, the role of the male is different than the female. When we enter a marriage, we are expected to fulfill the role of our gender. Again, this may be tough for us guys to fully realize. We are in the female position in this marriage! God impregnates us with His word and Spirit. He impregnates us with a calling and vision. We get pregnant! We give birth! We multiply! He is the stronger vessel. We do not impregnate God. He impregnates us.

In this marriage Jesus is the head. This is a biblical marriage. You got to learn to trust Him and follow His lead. You got to know your Husband's voice. You got to be able to pick your Husband's voice out of all the others that may be assaulting you, and any good wife should be able to do this. Hearing his voice is essential if we hope to live more in His supernatural ways rather than our own natural and mortal ways.

In an earthly marriage you have two imperfect people, now become one. However, in this supernatural marriage you have one who is perfect, and the other is not except through the perfection they legally receive in the marriage. You have one who really does know all, and one who only thinks they know all. You might wonder how it could be for such a marriage as this to work? Why would the perfect marry the desperately flawed? One is immortal and the other still mortal. It could *only* be love.

Herein we find another beauty, in that God promises by the time we reach that great wedding in the sky, we too will be perfected! And we too will be immortal. This will not be a marriage of the unequally yoked, but a marriage made in Heaven, perfectly balanced, perfectly fitted together, perfectly complete in every way.

Until then, we should rejoice that we have personal and close contact with the One who truly knows all! This is a superpower! Do we not see our great advantage? Why would we want to lead? Why would we want to lose our supernatural advantage? The lost man has none of this. Like Mary told those servants who needed wine, "Whatever He says, do it." Their obedience led to the best wine ever tasted. Our obedience will lead to our heart filled with joy, the best wine we ever tasted. He turns OUR water to HIS wine.

But then you might ask, why does the lost man seem to prosper so much in this world? Why am I not ruling and reigning? Well, first of all, many of them are greatly suffering. But for those who seem to be excelling and enjoying everything this world has to offer, this is all they have! For us it is not about money, but faith; and for us it is not about flesh, but Spirit.

Our treasures are eternal, and theirs are not. They will flourish for a little time. This is all they got for a little while, and then they are gone. We could name many, right? And remember, Esau sold his birthright for a pot of beans! Beans he pooped out on the ground twenty-four hours later! They can have the beans for now. I'll wait for heaven.

Did O.J. Simpson do it? Did he get away with murder? Many people believe he did. And for a few years, perhaps he did, but he died a few days ago. He died of cancer. Did he enjoy his beans? Does he realize now what a foolish trade he made? As he was dying of cancer, I wonder how highly he still esteemed his beans? Living in the beans. That stinks.

I'm sure he felt the time passed so quickly. And now he faces a judgement he cannot avoid, a judge and jury he cannot fool. If he did it, he hasn't gotten away with a thing. As a matter of fact, he multiplied his sin and judgement by lying, and being so arrogant as to believe he could escape his judgement. The foolish will always suffer more than the wise.

Now is a good time to consider the words of Solomon, perhaps the wisest man to ever live. I think words from such a man is worthy of consideration.

CHAPTER THREE

Is Jesus really a Knight in shining armor? Are we really a damsel in distress? Is there a dragon, an evil so dark as to boggle our mind to comprehend? When we see just how evil someone can be to another human being, for the sake of money or power or lust, can there be any doubt? We need saving from our self; the evil within us.

How can a person do something so horrible to another person when they would never want that done to themselves? Jesus was asked what is the greatest of the commandments. He was asked about a set of "commands", but His answer was a life of love, loving God and others. He answered a question about commands with an answer about loving.

> *"Jesus said to him, You shall love the Lord your God with all your heart, with all your soul, and with all your mind. This is the first and great commandment. And the second is like it: You shall love your neighbor as yourself. On these two commandments hang all the Law and the Prophets."*
>
> — Matthew 22:37-40 (NKJ)

In these two "loves", all is fulfilled. Agape love, the God kind of love, is the answer to it all. Jesus comes on this mission of love and righteousness to save us. He is a Knight in sacred armor, and when we gain His Name, we too are clothed in that armor of light! And He tells us to prepare our self in that armor daily, but do we? This is the supernatural way. Not doing it is the wilderness way. We gain His armor in His Name.

> *"Love does no harm to a neighbor; therefore, love is the fulfillment of the law. And do this, knowing the time, that now it is high time to awake out of sleep; for now our salvation is nearer than when we first believed. The night is far spent, the day is at hand. Therefore, let us cast off the works of darkness, <u>and let us put on the armor of light</u>."*
>
> — Romans 13:10-12 (KJV)
>
> *"<u>But put on the Lord Jesus Christ</u>, and make no provision for the flesh, to fulfill its lusts."*
>
> — Verse 14

Our Knight has a powerful Sword like none other, The Word of God! And as His Bride we too have that Sword to study and learn to use. But again, it's not a sword requiring great muscle to wield, it comes out of our mouth! It is powered by faith! It is a Sword like none-other! And it becomes our property as well as His in this great marriage. The Word is our Husband! We are married to the Word! Have you spent time with your Husband today? Have you pictured your salvation in this way?

Can we learn from earthly marriages things relating to Spirit? Of course we can; and should! Consider this, do we examine what our potential mate brings to the table if we marry? For example, if I am the potential wife, and I have hopes of my husband getting me into the music industry, such as a singer or musician, do I marry a man who is a great mechanic, but no skills in music?

Of course not, he has the wrong set of tools. Do not expect what he does not offer. If it's true love then it will not matter, but do not expect what he is not. Expect, learn, and enjoy what he is. What does your husband offer?

So, if I'm a woman who loves hot cars, this mechanic might be the man for me! He can teach me the skills. He has the tools and garage that would also now be mine. He has a love for working on cars. He has a hot car! Now I have a hot car! We have much we can enjoy together. We share a common passion. Not just a passion for each other, but also what we enjoy when together.

Now we must apply this to Christ. What set of tools does our Lord bring to the table? Not physical tools so much, but spiritual tools from a Sky Kingdom! A Sword that comes out of our mouth? Faith more than money? A life focused on Spirit more than flesh? Skills from a supernatural world? The way of eternal life? Yes, all this and more! But don't expect something from Him He is not.

Enter this marriage desiring to learn and to have what He is offering; and maximize your great opportunity! He's offering an eternal kingdom and release from the dragon. He's offering eternal gold, not temporary beans. He is all about Spirit, not beans. If you love beans, you'll be disappointed.

His Holy Spirit is in us to teach us the tools of His kingdom. But if we only have eyes for the things of this world, like looking back to Egypt, then once again, we are the Children of Israel in the wilderness. Our Husband can lead us to the Promised Land, a land of Spirit and faith, if we truly appreciate what He is offering. Don't keep crying for mammon (money), if He's offering mana, bread from heaven. Desire what you married. Be happy in what you married, for it is the greatest Kingdom of all!

What can Solomon show us in all this? His Trilogy of Books each have a very specific message. The first Book, Proverbs, is very logical, easy to understand, a lot of basic rules of life and wisdom. It is his foundational book. It is laying the general foundation for what comes in the next two, and few people disagree with the wisdoms of Proverbs. But the next two? Oh, now that is a different story. Even with his preparation book in our minds, we still struggle with those next two upward stair steps.

A lot of people don't like the second Book, Ecclesiastes; and many think the third Book should not be in the Bible at all! But that shows they don't understand at all, even though it is the highest wisdom. Be wary of these people. And if you're one of them, don't continue in that way. Climb higher and enter God's Sky Kingdom.

The three Books are also set up like the wilderness temple, in which you have the Outer Court, Proverbs; the Holy Place, Ecclesiastes; and the Holy of Holies, Song of Songs. You could say each book goes deeper and deeper, as well as higher and higher. Only God can do such things.

Many people get very uncomfortable with the Book of Ecclesiastes. Ecclesiastes is Jesus saying, *"Lay not up treasures in the earth, where moth and rust does corrupt, and thieves break in to steal. But lay up treasures for yourself in Heaven..."* Oh, a lot of people don't like Solomon calling our precious stuff nothing but dust in the wind, and vanity. If the passion of our life is built on these things, it hurts when Solomon calls it all a huge waste of time. What shall we live for then? How can we be happy without chasing material things? We are frustrated by the wisest man insinuating we are fools.

Ecclesiastes is like the linchpin of the three Books. Until you love the message there, and embrace its truth, you will struggle even more with Song of Songs. The Bible says be not entangled in this world, but so many of us are. Jesus even lived as a minimalist, and recommended it to the rich young ruler, but most of us walk away sad, like he did, because he had much stuff. Lot's wife just had to look back at all the stuff she was leaving, rather than obey God, and she was turned into a pillar of money. Salt was used as money, in that time.

A word to the wise, concerning the rapture, Jesus said, "*Remember Lot's wife.*"

You could say Ecclesiastes is a very negative and depressing Book. It is the opposite of the American Dream and American way, but it is the way of the Kingdom of God, it's not beans. You can't serve God and money. You can't be a good soldier of Jesus Christ and be entangled in this world. A heavy ship is first to sink, and Jesus said His burden was light and His yoke easy. That is not what many Christians seem to experience in their walk with Christ. Neither do they embrace Ecclesiastes. They are short circuiting the supernatural they could be enjoying, the light burden and easy yoke of our Lord.

Towards the end of Proverbs there are some scriptures that say this:

> *"There are three things that are too hard for me, really four I don't understand: the way an eagle flies in the sky, the way a snake slides over a rock, the way a ship sails on the ocean, and the way a man and a woman fall in love."*
>
> — Proverbs 30:18-19

This is the Book of Proverbs. It has much to say about marriage, avoiding adultery and prostitutes. It is a Book full of great wisdom, understanding of God, basics of life, but how does falling in love happen? A mystery.

However, by the time he is writing Song of Songs, he may not understand it, but he certainly believes in it. Every follower of Christ should have a firm grip of the three Books the man gifted from God with wisdom wrote. Who would deny that? And hopefully, we will grow to understand and embrace all three.

If you're okay with Proverbs but struggle with Ecclesiastes, you're probably still in the wilderness. Song of Songs is the Promised Land, and it is the Holy of Holies. In the Old Covenant, only the High Priest could enter the Holy of Holies, and only once a year on the high holy day, and at risk of his own death.

But here again, our Husband, our Knight in sacred armor has ripped the veil in two that once divided the Holy from the Holy of Holies, and in Jesus Name we have full access to that place 24/7! But not without His Name. No other Name. Not Buddha, Mohamad, or your praying Grandma.

You and I were never strong enough to rip that veil open. But our Husband is very strong. He is so much stronger than we are, and also the dragon. The dragon suffered such an embarrassing defeat when our Lord came up out of that grave that day! The dragon knows his days are numbered. His fear and anger increases, the closer he gets to his judgement.

But let's focus on Ecclesiastes and Song of Songs. As said before, most people get along pretty well with Proverbs. Even some unbelievers enjoy Proverbs. But God is calling His Bride to the High Places, a Sky Kingdom, not this earthbound land of mortality and natural ways.

CHAPTER FOUR

Ecclesiastes, where do we begin?

> *"These are the words of the Quester, David's son and king in Jerusalem: Smoke, nothing but smoke. (That's what the Quester says.) There's nothing to anything – it's all smoke. What's there to show for a lifetime of work, a lifetime of working your fingers to the bone?"*
>
> —Ecclesiastes 1:1 (Message Bible)

How's that for a start? That is a taste of Ecclesiastes, written by possibly the wisest man, other than Christ, to ever live. And as much as you may not like it, or want to think about it, we know it is true, don't we. And that bothers us even more. It is our mortality, the curse of our mortality, and if we live in denial, our ending will be sad indeed, as we leave behind all the "stuff" we worked so hard and long to get. We die questioning, what was it all about? Is this all there is?

There's a place in Memphis Tennessee you can go and gawk at all the stuff Elvis left behind. For a fee you can see it. Very sad, really. We spend our whole life working hard, chasing dreams, collecting as many of our desires as we can, knowing the whole time that we leave it all in the end. That's the book of Ecclesiastes.

Is this all there is?

We may question this even before death, but we press on. Unfortunately, for all the unbelievers, they will die, cross to the other side, and discover this is not all there is. This is only a tiny tip of a huge iceberg known as God!

Solomon has studied, learned, pondered all this and is now proclaiming, "There is more! But it's not here! It's there!" Don't blow the "there" on the smoke and mirrors of "here!" Don't sell your birthright for a pot of beans! This is what the wisest man declares to be true.

Solomon certainly did not live as a minimalist, and when his reign was over, he had a power- hungry son who led Israel into great division, a great split! Solomon left Israel poised for disaster. We can be so wise that we know what the truth is, and still fail to live it. The ripple effect of our life affects many generations to come, whether to the good, or the bad. Let us be of those who overcome evil with good.

Solomon sounds very sad and frustrated in Ecclesiastes. Is he realizing the sadness of his own plight? A life spent in great wealth and luxury, and for what? Did he realize bad things were coming? Did he look at his own children and see the bad coming? But too late to undo it now?

> "Call me 'the Quester.' I've been king over Israel in Jerusalem. I looked most carefully into everything, searched out all that is done on this earth. And let me tell you, there's not much to write home about. God hasn't made it easy for us. I've seen it all and it's nothing but smoke – smoke, and spitting into the wind."

> "Life's a corkscrew that can't be straightened, a minus that won't add up."

> "I said to myself, I know more and I'm wiser than anyone before me in Jerusalem. I've stockpiled wisdom and knowledge. What I've finally concluded is that so-called wisdom and knowledge are mindless and witless – nothing but spitting into the wind."

> "Much learning earns you much trouble. The more you know, the more you hurt."

> "I said to myself, Let's go for it – experiment with pleasure, have a good time! But there was nothing to it, nothing but smoke."

"What do I think of the fun-filled life? Insane! Insane! My verdict on the pursuit of happiness? Who needs it? With the help of a bottle of wine and all the wisdom I could muster, I tried my level best to penetrate the absurdity of life. I wanted to get a handle on anything useful we mortals might do during the years we spend on this earth."

— Ecclesiastes 1:12-18 & 2:1-3 (Message Bible)

"Then I took a good look at everything I had done, looked at all the sweat and hard work. But when I looked, I saw nothing but smoke. Smoke and spitting into the wind. There was nothing to any of it. Nothing."

"And then I took a hard look at what's smart and what's stupid. What's left to do after you've been king? That's a hard act to follow. You just do what you can, and that's it. But I did see that it is better to be smart than stupid, just as light is better than darkness. Even so, though the smart ones see where they're going and the stupid ones grope in the dark, they're all the same in the end. One fate for all – and that's it."

"When I realized that my fate is the same as the fool's, I had to ask myself, So why bother being wise? It's all smoke, nothing but smoke. The smart and the stupid both disappear out of sight. In a day or two they're both forgotten.

Yes, both the smart and the stupid die, and that's it."

"I hate life. As far as I can see, what happens on earth is bad business. It's smoke – and spitting into the wind." — VRS 11-17

One point Solomon made of great interest to me is, the more you see and understand, the more you hurt. Is this good or bad? Personally, I think it is good. If we ignore the reality of this mortal life and the pain people go through, we become heartless and selfish individuals. As an American, I've never known the hunger others have suffered through in many poorer countries. If we don't ask the questions of why am I fed to the full, but they starve to death? If we ignore such questions and offer no help to the hurting and helpless, what kind of person have I become? And how will I answer God on my judgement day?

We act as if for some reason we deserved to have it so much better. We throw plates of food away while others swallow gravel and grass trying to dull the hunger pains, and we do nothing? Yes, what Solomon saw made him very sad, as it should us all. Hopefully even sad enough to be moved by the love of God to take less our self, so someone else, who has nothing, can have a little more. Less can be more.

If these thoughts make you uncomfortable, then you will never understand, or graduate to the book, Song of Songs. You may think you have. You may tell yourself you've embraced the book, Song of Songs, but the Bible ask the question, how can I love God and yet hate my brother or sister? (Or leave them suffering, if I can help. The more Solomon saw, the more it hurt.)

No, Solomon's wisdom is too great for us to outsmart. We are guilty. If we want to live in the Promised Land of God's Spirit, then we've got to embrace the book of Ecclesiastes on our way to getting there. God calls us into the high places of life in the book of Song of Songs. Our Lover is seen skipping across the tops of mountains as He calls us to join him in the high places. He skips upon those peaks like a gazelle, Solomon declares.

So… when you look in the mirror, do you see a materialistic person? How much of your life is focused on money in one form or another? Do you worry about your retirement? Bank account? Having enough? Man-made ways of trying to build your wealth, store it in barns? It's all wilderness thinking. Solomon declared it all insanity and dust in the wind! *And Jesus asked us to consider the birds.*

So…if we are wise…we understand Ecclesiastes stands in our way of Song of Songs, just as the wilderness stood in the way of the Promised Land. Now we have a better picture of change needing to occur in us, if we ever hope to know God's BEST. Let us focus on laying up treasures in heaven, as our Lord has said. This way, we are moving towards gaining all our treasures, and not moving towards leaving all of them. Just ask Elvis.

CHAPTER FIVE

So how does Ecclesiastes conclude? Are we left with a very sad ending and no hope? Not really, Solomon finally finds his way to the only possible happy ending to this mortal life. Here is his final conclusion in Ecclesiastes. I specifically point out "in Ecclesiastes", because his next book has so much joy and hope to offer. Did he finally see the big picture?

> "Life, lovely while it lasts, is soon over. Life as we know it, precious and beautiful, ends. The body is put back in the same ground it came from. The spirit returns to God, who first breathed it."

> "It's all smoke, nothing but smoke. The Quester says that everything's smoke."

> "Besides being wise himself, the Quester also taught others knowledge. He weighed, examined, and arranged many proverbs. The Quester did his best to find the right words and write the plain truth."

"The words of the wise prod us to live well. They're like nails hammered home, holding life together. They are given by God, the one Shepherd."

"But regarding anything beyond this, dear friend, go easy. There's no end to the publishing of books, and constant study wears you out so you're no good for anything else. The last and final word is this: Fear God. Do what He tells you."

"And that's it. Eventually God will bring everything that we do out into the open and judge it according to its hidden intent, whether it's good or evil."

— Ecclesiastes 12: 6-14 (Message Bible)

And that, my friends, is how Ecclesiastes ends. Note that at the end of this book, Solomon's admonition is based on "fear". In Proverbs, Solomon's own words teach us that fear of God is the "beginning" of wisdom. Yes, this is where it all starts. Fear of God. And rightly so! But once we fall in love with Jesus, God's word says love fulfills the law. We do not live a life of fear if we love our Lord. True love will carry us much farther than fear. Love overcomes fear, as Solomon's next book describes in ways that make a lot of people uncomfortable.

As we enter Song of Songs, I want to walk through the scriptural doorway of Isaiah 53: 2b-3 (KJV):

> *"He has no form or comeliness; and when we see Him, **there is no beauty that we should desire Him.** He is despised and rejected by men, a Man of sorrows and acquainted with grief. And we hid, as it were, our faces from Him; He was despised, and we did not esteem Him."*

The ways of our Lord are not esteemed by many. As a matter of fact, there are many who downright hate Him. But what causes you to be different and see His beauty? What causes you to be different from the lustful masses of humanity who see no beauty in Him? For the book, Song of Songs, is all about seeing His beauty and falling in love.

Isaiah emphasized the point that He had no form of beauty to them. Even as His love carried Him through the torturous beating with the cat-of-nine-tails in order to save us, we did not see His beauty. All we saw was a man turned to hamburger, seemingly unable to defend Himself, and on his way to a horrible death. Who would want any part of that? Who would want to risk the chance to end up like Him, even though they knew the lame had walked through this man, the blind had seen, the sick healed, demons cast out, and even the dead raised to life, *through this man.*

They ignored all that beauty as they were consumed in fear, hate, and love of money. Many of them had been bribed that day, to shout for His execution while a real criminal was set free. They saw no comeliness, no beauty in Him to cause desire, and yet the tables would suddenly turn and this weak and dying man would change the whole world, because of His beauty that some of us recognize and honor.

If you have read this far, something has kept you going. You are not turned off by the idea of being married to Jesus. Something is causing you to keep an open mind on the matter and consider its possibilities. And the deeper we go in this book, the more we will be using "marriage" as our teaching tool for understanding what it truly means to be "saved."

You went forward at a Church, or someone led you to Jesus, as they say, at work, at home, in the streets, wherever. It can happen anywhere if you are sincere. You admitted you're a sinner by nature, and you asked God/Jesus to save you, and change you. Now they say you are "born-again". And if you were true, then indeed you are, born-again into a new life! But how can you get the quickest understanding of what this means? I recommend understanding it as a biblical marriage to God; for according to scripture, that is what it is!

That understanding alone, can get you off on the right foot with God in your new relationship. I specify "biblical" marriage because the ungodly world of man has many variations of what they call marriage. God does not. It is a union of devotion and faithfulness between one male (man) and female (woman). Sex outside of marriage is sin. Sex is for a married couple. Sex with anyone other than your spouse is sin.

The man is given the final say in the marriage, but he is to love his wife so much that there is no worry of him dominating her, or not considering her opinion and desires. He loves her so much that it pains him when she is not happy. He may be the head, but he loves her so much he will also serve her whenever possible. Her welfare, and the welfare of the family will be his utmost consideration in every decision they make. And a God-seeking man will do his best to get his direction from God, Himself. The man is not the ultimate head of the marriage, God is. The man answers directly to God. You could say he's a middleman.

Sadly, there are many today who have never even seen a good marriage. They've seen anger, pain, fear, and abuse. They've seen broken marriages, divorce, and abandoned children. They've seen everything under the sun except what God set as marriage. This might be a disadvantage for you, but at least you know some things *not* to do, right?

As you study your Bible, go to a good Church, read this book, your understanding will grow rapidly, and God's Holy Spirit will be helping you, working from within. You have become the temple of the Holy Spirit, God Himself, the Spirit of Christ. You are now one with Christ! That is what biblical marriage teaches. We will go through difficult times, but we don't just go through them, we "grow" through them, and we are not alone. He is with us. Our Husband is with us.

Ecclesiastes gives us the bleak picture of what life offers if you only live in this physical world. It is the house built on sand, as our Husband described, whos' ending is destruction, a great fall. It is a dead-end street, and we all wrestle with the sadness of that. But Song of Songs is the house built on the Rock of Christ Jesus, life without end! His house, which is now OUR house, will never fall. That is what our Husband has promised us. That is part of the package that comes with His Name and Ring on our spiritual finger. His Ring overcomes them all! Even death itself.

There are no perfect marriages in this earth, but in Heaven it will be. Let's take a quick peak at that before we examine Solomon's Song of Songs.

> *"Then Death and Hades were cast into the lake of fire. This is the second death. And anyone not found written in the Book of Life was cast into the lake of fire."*

> *"Now I saw a new heaven and a new earth, for the first heaven and the first earth had passed away. Also there was no more sea. Then I, John, saw the holy city, New Jerusalem, coming down out of heaven from God, **prepared as a bride adorned for her husband.** And I heard a loud voice from heaven saying, Behold, the tabernacle of God is with men, and He will dwell with them, and they shall be His people. God Himself will be with them and be their God. And God will wipe away every tear from their eyes; there shall be no more death, nor sorrow, nor crying. There shall be no more pain, for the former things have passed away."*

> — Revelation 20:14-15 & 21:1-4 (NKJV)

> *"I, Jesus, have sent My angel to testify to you these things in the churches. I am the Root and the Offspring of David, the Bright and Morning Star."*

> *"**And the Spirit and the bride say, Come!** And let him who hears say, Come! And let him who thirsts come. Whoever desires, let him take of the water of life freely."*
>
> *— Revelation 22: 16-17*

Yes, this is a real marriage in heaven. If you still have any doubts, let these words remove them all!

> *"And I heard, as it were, the voice of a great multitude, as the sound of many waters and as the sound of mighty thunderings, saying, Alleluia! For the Lord God Omnipotent reigns! Let us be glad and rejoice and give Him glory, **for the marriage of the Lamb has come, and His wife has made herself ready.** And to her it was granted to be arrayed in fine linen, clean and bright, for the fine linen is the righteous acts of the saints."*
>
> *"Then he said to me, Write: Blessed are those who are called **to the marriage supper of the Lamb!** And he said to me, These are the true sayings of God."* — Revelation 19: 6-9

With these thoughts in mind, let's enjoy the book of Song of Songs!

CHAPTER SIX

"The Lord God is my strength (heavy lifter); He
will make my feet like deer's feet, and He will
make me walk on my high hills."

— Habakkuk 3:19 (NKJ)

The above scripture is not from Song of Songs but confirms the same message. Song of Songs is a call to leave the lower lands of Ecclesiastes and enter the high places of Christ, our Lord and Husband. There is a reason why I like to refer to God's Kingdom as a Sky Kingdom. Jesus said to seek those things which are ABOVE! He constantly calls us to the high places of Spirit, and to crucify the low places of flesh.

In His great Sermon on the Mount, He challenges us to consider the birds. These winged creatures with the power of flight, and they do not worry about where their next meal is coming from. When I considered the birds, as Jesus said to do, it led me to the list of clean and unclean birds identified in the Old Covenant, and I was surprised what I learned there! There are treasures of understanding to be found in considering birds.

God's Kingdom is all about lifting us "up," not putting us down. In Song of Songs our Lord is depicted as coming across the mountain tops like a gazelle! He is calling His Bride, His love, to join Him there. He will give me feet like the gazelle to live in the high places, or wings like the eagle to mount "up"! But these are supernatural abilities that only come in the Promised Land of seeking God's Holy Spirit, not in the dry lands of the wilderness.

It is such a tragedy, a tragedy beyond description that so many Christians fail to ever leave the wilderness. They do not consider the message God has painted for us with the birds. They live earth-bound lives constantly stressed out in worry and fear over... what? Money most of the time. Things related to money. Instead of simple childlike faith in our Lord.

The book of Revelation speaks of "our first love". Sony and Cher made famous a song, "I Got You, Babe". It spoke of all the things they did not have, not even money to pay the rent, but they had each other. It is a song of being what I call, love drunk, our first love.

"Nevertheless I have this against you, that you have left your first love. Remember therefore from where you have fallen; ...

— Revelation 2: 4-5a (KJV)

I remember when I first fell in love with a beautiful young lady who eventually became my wife. I would have followed her anywhere. I probably still would today, after forty-eight years of marriage, but I do have a little more sense in my head now, and perhaps think more clearly. However, my Lord is perfect, and I should want to follow Him anywhere! I should have no fear of where He leads. In fact, I should greatly desire those places, as if I were still in that love drunk first love.

In Song of Songs, we see a romance building between the Lord and His future Bride. He courts us to win our affections. He is our valiant Knight saving us from the great dragon. We begin falling in love with who He is and everything He offers in His Name, but will we leave the low places of this earthly life and follow Him into the mountains, and even into the sky? Will we learn to flap less, and soar more? There's a lot of flapping that goes on in the wilderness.

Not everything is peaches and cream in the romance of Song of Songs. The Shulamite lady, representing us and the Church, sometimes struggles with what her Lover is asking of her. She goes through some hard times, but her overwhelming desire for her Lover eventually pulls her through and draws them together, forever. It has a happy ending. But it is love that draws her, not fear.

Some Christians are still hung up in the Law, of which Christ has set us free. He is calling us to a love relationship, not a law relationship. Jesus said, he who the Son sets free, is free indeed. I don't know if this makes sense to everyone, but it means something to me. It occurred to me the other day, that when a man and woman marry, all their other relatives become "In-laws".

The mother becomes the mother-in-law. Father equals father-in-law. They now have brother and sisters-in-law, etc. and etc. But the wife is not called wife-in-law. I pondered this. It's their love for each other that makes the difference, as far as I'm concerned. All the other relatives are simply now related by law, but a love resulting in marriage creates a "oneness" that supersedes the legal contract of marriage. They are ONE. These two would have become one, because of their love for each, whether any law was involved or not.

Maybe that makes sense, or maybe not. Maybe that means something to you, or not. It does to me. The Old Covenant laws could never have produced the "oneness" God was going for. No "wife-in-law" was going to be good enough. Only the love of God can create the kind of oneness known as husband and wife.

King David is an example of what we're trying to explain. When he had committed such grievous sin and was crying out in repentance for forgiveness. How did he know God was not looking for him to fulfill the law?

David lived during the time of the Old Covenant with all the laws and sacrifices that went with it. David's sins were so grievous you would think God would be requiring him to do every single letter of the law to seek his forgiveness, and yet, David somehow understood that was not what God wanted, as recorded in Psalms 51:16 (KJV):

> *"For You do not desire sacrifice, or else I would give it; You do not delight in burnt offering, the sacrifices of God are a broken spirit, a broken and contrite heart – These, O God, You will not despise."*

How did David know this? I'm sure if he had gone to the religious leaders and experts of his time, they would not have known what David knew. They would have instructed him in all the ways of the law, and yet David, a once simple shepherd boy, understood more than they. It could be said he already understood what would come, Jesus Christ, by way of Judah, not Levi.

We are living in such a time now. Jesus, who lived and recommended minimalism as a way of life, is twisted into a pretzel recommending materialism! I'm sorry, but the young rich man walked away sad that day! And when Jesus could have ridden a stallion, He chose a donkey! How many examples should I list? Consider the birds? Lay not up treasures in earth? How many do you want? No place to lay His head? The Apostles gave up everything to follow Him? The list is huge! But today's religious "experts" teach different.

How our experts try to force old wine into the new wine skin is beyond me. How do they not understand? God has so far separated us from the Old Covenant of our spiritual death, that He made sure Jesus was not even born of the tribe of Levi, so that it would actually be spiritually illegal for Him to be of that old priesthood system. Jesus set us free from all that, and He is of the Tribe of Judah, for which we give Him praise! (Judah means praise.) All praise and honor is His. None of it is ours. Our works do nothing but fail!

Interesting note: John the Baptist, the prophet called to prepare the way for Christ, was the son of a Levite priest, and yet he never ministered in the temple. As the forerunner of Christ Himself, God called him away from the priesthood at that time and into the wilderness, a place of solitude and separation, to hear the whispers of God.

Even in our Lord's forerunner, we can see God separating from that old Covenant of the Levite priesthood. God completed it in Christ. First, He completed the fulfillment of every law, even down to the least jot and title. Then He finished that dispensation through Christ, set us free from the law, and established a way of grace through faith. This way of grace literally separated from the Tribe of Levi and into the Tribe of Judah, praise!

In the marriage we receive the benefits of having fulfilled the law even though we have not. Our Husband, whom we are one with, fulfilled the law for us and it is as if we fulfilled it too, because "His fulfilling" is also ours! What is His has become mine! Is God some kind of genius or what?

My personal opinion is, anyone rejecting grace through marriage to Christ, is not set free from the law, but will be judged by the law on that day. God's laws are still valid and true. Sin is still sin and man is still fallen in sin. We are spared from the condemnation we deserve and have earned only by way of mercy and grace in Christ, through faith. We believed God's word, fell in love, and entered marriage to Christ Jesus.

With that in mind, the law still gets fulfilled as best we can, because God's love working in us is the perfection of the law. For example, a pet peeve of mine is people get all hung up on a ten percent tithe, but I say, what is God laying on your heart to give? The New Covenant is a circumcision of the heart. It might be a lot more than ten percent. Love always out-performs law. God's love in us will motivate us to give without any ten percent law needed.

Remember, God looks at our heart and delights in the "cheerful" giver. Does law promote a cheerful giver? Feeling forced to do something never promotes cheerfulness. Jesus rescued us from the duties of law and planted us in the rich soil of His love. In the rich soil of praise!

Oh boy, dare I touch this subject? I guess I have already. Does this even belong in a book about being the Bride of the Lamb, Lord? But who is this person we have married? What is He really like? I may not be able to explain it, but my gut says this does need shared. I share this at this time with reluctance, because this could get this book banned in Churches, but I feel I must. I risk the acceptance of all my hard work here, but I must write as God moves me to write. So much time and work to write these words, and I put it all at risk? Yes, Lord.

So, I do caution the reader, in case I'm wrong, as my own studied opinion based on my own logic and how I have felt led of the Lord, I must be honest. If you think I'm wrong, please do not allow this to erase all the knowledge and vision you have enjoyed thus far, and likely will also unto the end of this book. But here's my honest thoughts concerning tithing. The law of tithing is of the Old Covenant, it is of the law, and Jesus set us free. It does not belong in the new wineskin, the precious marriage Covenant of our Lord, Jesus the Messiah.

> *"And verily they that are of the sons of Levi, who receive the office of the priesthood, have a <u>commandment</u> to take tithes of the people according to the <u>law</u>..."*— Hebrews 7:5a (KJV)

The above scripture plainly identifies tithing as a "commandment" and of the "law". There are those who try to teach otherwise, saying it preceded the law when Abraham gave a tenth to Melchizedek. Even if it did, it still comes across as a law and is identified as such in Hebrews. Stealing is against the law.

I was raised from a child to tithe. I was raised Baptist. Tithing was like my bread and butter of spiritual understanding. One thing I knew for sure, if I didn't give ten percent back to God, I was robbing God! (Not a smart thing to do. Also, fear and shame invoking.)

But I was also taught there is no Baptism in the Holy Spirit. Later, some very devout people began showing me different. This opened a whole new world to me. But still, even most of them preach tithing. Even the Church I attend now. I have been unable to find a Church who does not. So, maybe I'm wrong, but I must be honest even if wrong.

When I began seeing something different, I must admit I was very surprised. I've checked and triple checked this so many times that my head spins. So, I share these thoughts, but only you can decide if you agree. Here we go.

In the book of Acts they were giving ALL! Teaching tithing would have actually brought in less! Love outperforms law. Did they have to? Were they being forced or shamed into it? No, the story of Ananias and Sapphira makes that clear. In fact, let's look at that for a moment.

> *"But a man named Ananias — his wife, Sapphira, conniving in this with him — sold a piece of land, secretly kept part of the price for himself, and then brought the rest to the Apostles and made an offering of it. "*

> *"Peter said, Ananias, how did Satan get you to lie to the Holy Spirit and secretly keep back part of the price of the field? Before you sold it, it was all yours, **and after you sold it, the money was yours to do with as you wished.** So what got into you to pull a trick like this? You didn't lie to men but to God. "*
>
> *"Ananias, when he heard those words, fell down dead."* — Acts 5: 1-5a. (Message Bible)

Basically, the same thing happened to his wife when she came in later. But we should note a couple things. One, Ananias was not in trouble for wanting to keep part of the money for himself. He was in trouble for "lying" about it.

Peter even told him the money was "his" and he was free to do with it "whatever" he wanted. And note: Peter did *not* say after giving God's ten percent, then you are free to do as you want with the other ninety percent. If the tithe were still in effect, that is what Peter should have instructed. Would he be so careless in such a matter? The Word of God is not known to be careless in important matters. And if it is law, you're really not free to do as you wish. Breaking the law will land you in a prison, whether spiritual or physical.

And I know, again, "experts" try to say the tithe is not part of the law, that it preceded the law in that Abraham gave a tenth to Melchizedek before the law ever appeared with Moses. This is true, but the tithe as we describe it is still described as a "law", because you are taking God's portion. You are "stealing" from God. Theft is against the law. Hebrews 7:5 confirms the tithe as part of the law.

Has Jesus set us free from every law except money? Is His grace not powerful enough to overcome the love of money in us? The Church of Acts sure seemed to have no problem. We can be trusted in everything except money? The tithe is God's one exception from all the other laws He set us free from? Does that make any logical sense?

Or does it make more sense that what has become a very materialistic Church would be afraid to let go of the law of the tithe? The obvious love of money we see in so many of our preachers and people as they build personal empires for the lost to drive by and gawk at. Not only the Church buildings, but their own personal homes. Do we see a likely connection here? Do we see potential motive? These buildings and homes are not cheap.

And what about the law of circumcision? That law went all the way back to Abraham also, and the Bible makes plain it is no more. For some reason these tithe preaching pastors do not bring up circumcision at the same time they say tithe goes all the way back to Abraham. The fact this is rarely ever brought up is highly suspicious, to say the least. Again, does this reveal motive? Perhaps motive they are not even aware of themselves, but a good detective always looks for potential motive to solve a crime. Are we living fully in the circumcised heart?

And what about every mention of money and giving in the New Covenant is always as an "offering", not a tithe. Did the New Testament writers simply stop using the word, tithe? They just dropped that word from their vocabulary for some odd reason? It's just a strange coincidence? I see it as an intentional statement. When the word tithe is used it's in reference to when the New Covenant was still not in effect.

So, as far as what Jesus said to the Pharisees, who were still under the law at that time, and Jesus had not established the New Covenant yet? Well, that was the only correct answer He could have given them at that time. Those Pharisees were still under the law. Surely this is easily seen. Are you telling me you don't see this? The very fact you don't mention this in your sermon is also highly suspicious. You talk about the words being in red, but no mention of the New Covenant not yet in effect? And your motive is?

So why are so many of our religious leaders and experts still preaching a law of tithing? Do they have a love of money? Do they have a lack of faith? Have they not read the book of Hebrews? Do they realize they are trying to force old wine into the new wineskin? Why do they do this? We are not of Levi; we are of Judah.

What possible motives could there be? Only a few exist, and of those, a lack of understanding would be the least offensive, in my opinion. But are they not the experts who have gone to college and have the degrees? David learned more tending sheep in quiet places than all they.

I do not say these things to hurt anybody, but Jesus set us free from the old law and lifted us to much higher places, and we should not be forcing old wine into the new wineskin. God's love is the fulfillment of the law. Love needs no laws. We learn this in first Timothy one, beginning in verse five.

> *"Now the end of the commandment is charity (love) out of a pure heart, and of a good conscience, and of faith unfeigned:"* (KJV)

> *"The whole point of what we're urging is simply love — love uncontaminated by self-interest and counterfeit faith, a life open to God."*

> *"Those who fail to keep to this point soon wander off into dead ends of gossip. They set themselves up as experts on religious issues, but haven't the remotest idea of what they are holding forth with such imposing eloquence."*
>
> *"It's true that moral guidance and counsel need to be given, but the way you say it and to whom you say it are as important as what you say. **<u>It's obvious, isn't it, that the law code isn't for people who live responsibly, but for the irresponsible, who defy all authority,</u>** riding roughshod over God, life, sex, truth, whatever! They are cynical toward the great message I've been put in charge of by this great God."*
>
> *— (Message Bible)*

We could say the law was for the yet spiritually immature, which is what we are before coming to Christ. Children need rules to keep them in line, but Paul said when he became a man, he put away childish things. A mature Christian operates by the love of God, hears God's voice, and obeys. A mature child of God has the ability to live this way. One more scripture:

> *"**<u>But before faith came</u>**, we were kept under the law, shut up unto the faith which should afterwards be revealed. Wherefore the law was our **<u>schoolmaster</u>** (like children) to bring us unto Christ, that we might be justified by faith.*

> But after that faith is come, __we are no longer__
> __under a schoolmaster.__" *(i.e. the law.)*
>
> — Galatians 3: 23-25

It plainly says we are no longer, no longer under the schoolmaster of the law, like little children too immature to know and do right. That has ended for us. Jesus was of Judah, not Levi. Jesus fulfilled every letter of the law, for us, and then established salvation through grace and faith, a circumcision of the heart. I have studied these scriptures every way I know how, and this is the only way it all makes sense to me. Whether my book is blacklisted by the Church or not, I must be honest in what I believe, as must we all.

So, with these things in mind, what does the New Testament, "our" Covenant, say about "giving"? What does it "actually" say? What words does it "actually" use? We can start with some words in red, where Paul quoted Jesus as saying:

> *"It is more blessed to give than to receive."*
>
> — Acts 20:35 (KJV)

This is what Jesus said. Christians are called to be givers. For some it is even their special gifting. If we have entered God's love, then what does ten percent have to do with it? How does that even make any sense? When you're moved by love, are you calculating the numbers? Do you need to calculate numbers? Do you even care? Did the widow calculate numbers with her widow's mite? Love gives to the best they can. Love is extravagant. We can be love-drunk and give ridiculously. It is more blessed to be givers rather than takers.

I've heard Uber drivers say they like picking up drunk people because they sometimes pay them ridiculous amounts for the ride. Can you believe it? But it does make sense. If we are love-drunk, we're not worried about ten percent. We probably are too drunk to even begin to calculate it.

When a famine was hitting an area, they did this:

> *"Then the disciples, every man <u>according to his ability</u>, determined to send relief to the brethren which dwelt in Judea."* — Acts 11:29 (KJV)

> *"Now concerning the collection for the saints, as I have given order to the churches of Galatia, even so do ye."*

> *"Upon the first day of the week let every one of you lay by him in store, <u>as God hath prospered him</u>, that there be no gatherings when I come."*
>
> — 1ˢᵗ Corinthians 16:1-2 (KJV)

I will end with this one because in my mind this gives the clearest and most logical explanation of New Covenant giving.

> *"But this I say, He which soweth sparingly shall reap also sparingly; and he that soweth bountifully shall reap also bountifully."*
>
> *"Every man according as he purposeth in his heart, so let him give; not grudgingly, or of necessity: for God loveth a cheerful giver."*
>
> — 2nd Corinthians 9:6-7 (KJV)

I chose to use King James version in the hope of lessening suspicion of manipulation. If I have missed something in the New Covenant of Christ, or my logic and understanding fails to hold up, please let me know. I have no desire to misinterpret God's Word. I gain nothing from doing so.

I was truly tempted NOT to put it in here, knowing it might close the doors for me on many Churches. I would love to see this little book go forth abundantly into God's Kingdom in this earth. I would love to have opportunities to teach and share in many Churches. I put all that at risk in sharing what I have shared. What selfish motive would I have to sabotage the prospects of my own book in such a way? But I say again, God's people are called to be givers, even as God **"<u>so loved</u>"** the world that He **"<u>gave</u>"**.

Perhaps to endanger my prospects even more, I'll say this quickly and move on. America is a falling nation because the Church became a money and materialistic hungry machine who lost the power of God. Jesus lived as a minimalist and warned against the love of money. He plainly stated you cannot serve God and money; but look at all the wealthy preachers today who preach the American dream rather than the Kingdom of God.

And it's not just the preachers. We the people love that message. We love the idea of the American Dream, but have you noticed it is getting harder to have the American Dream without selling your soul? A great danger lies in this! What has happened to this once great country?

I believe we are now in the prayer of Elijah, and nothing is going to change that unless the Church gets right with God and returns to her first love. There are a lot of priests of Baal that need to be slain by God's true prophets. No President is going to fix this. Only a God-anointed Church can, and so far, I don't see that happening.

Elijah prayed for the land to be cursed, to become dry like the desert, the wilderness, and God answered his prayer. Might we be in such a time now? Have we become so worldly that it has come to this? I'm watching closely. The jury is still out. But we soon shall see.

If we are in the prayer of Elisha, then no matter who we elect, no matter how much they may seem capable of fixing it all, no matter what great promises they may make, it will still be cursed. It will still turn out to be cursed, leading to more bad things. Only God's Bride getting back right with her Husband, returning to a true love of His words and ways, will begin turning this great ship around. And a large ship turns slowly.

In this election coming up, (I'm writing this on April 7th, 2024), we have three choices for President. I believe all three will bring a different judgement from God. I believe all three to be judgement coming. Another time David got in trouble with God, he was given three choices. All three were bad! All three were judgements! But God was allowing David to choose the judgement. And so shall we on election day. This is all recorded in Second Samuel 24: 10-13.

In my opinion, we are still too far from what was the original way of Church that Jesus established, and the early Apostles continued. And part of that was keeping it simple. It's hard to stop something as simple as what Jesus started. Its simplicity is part of its beauty. With God, less really does become more.

Roman Emperor Constantine, be he truly Christian or not, should never have been allowed to have as much say in Church matters as he had. Let me ask this, how many of you think we will still be able to meet in these beautiful huge buildings, our Churches, as this country continues slipping into more and more ungodliness?

Is your Church at least preparing for what we can plainly see coming down the tracks of our future? Every Church should be putting a heavy emphasis on Home Groups/ Small Groups as much as possible. Those who are awake can surely see the handwriting on the wall.

According to our worldly government and the laws of our land, our Bible is a book of Hate Speech and potential terrorism. They say we support something called Nationalism, and we're racist, but they are developing a one-world government, and we are in the way. The handwriting is on the wall. How much time do we still have? Are we ready? Are our big expensive buildings ready for all-out war? No, they are not. They simply make easy to hit… and hard to miss… TARGETS.

How have we slid so far that the Book most people believed in during the time of our country becoming the super-power of the earth, we now declare to be Hate Speech and can get you thrown in jail? Do you need any more proof of the judgement on this nation? Do you still believe we are the super-power? Or do you see our judgement happening? Our days of being "blessed" numbered. And what is the solution? More politics? LOL.

This nation needs a return to a love of God and His Word in the earth. That will change everything. That will change the politicians who are in office, and the judges who preside over courts. That will change the average person in the streets, and what the American Dream should be. Only God can change our selfish hearts of stone back to hearts of love and wisdom.

Are we ready for Song of Songs now?

> *"Kiss me—full on the mouth! Yes! For your love is better than wine, headier than your aromatic oils. The syllables of your name murmur like a meadow brook. No wonder everyone loves to say your name!"*
>
> — Song of Songs 1: 2-3 (Message Bible) (*Everything is in His Name. All of heaven is in His Name. We need His Name!)*
>
> *"Take me away with you! Let's run off together! An elopement with my King Lover! We'll celebrate, we'll sing, we'll make great music. Yes! For your love is better than vintage wine. Everyone loves you – of course! And why not?"*
>
> — VRS 4 (Message Bible)

Song of Songs is a book of great passion. Surely, those first words were a shock, like a punch to the gut, in contrast to what we had just been discussing. We understand such passion over some man or woman we may have feelings toward, but do we get uncomfortable when we apply that to God? Granted, it's not a flesh-based passion for God, but David said his soul longed after God like a deer pants for a water brook! Does our vision of God stir such feelings in us? This scripture is saying "Take me away with You!"

This is how Song of Songs begins, like a romance off to the races! However, a note of concern suddenly enters the picture in the very next lines. In 1:6 we read:

> *"Don't look down on me because I'm dark, darkened by the sun's harsh rays. My brothers ridiculed me and sent me to work in the fields. They made me care for the face of the earth, but I had no time to care for my own face."*

Suddenly, our Shulamite woman seems very concerned about her darkness of skin. Is that not a perfect picture of us? We love the thought of running after the Lord with all our heart and complete abandon, but what about our dark side? The flesh still hanging to us, pulling us down and saying you're not good enough. And trapped in those thoughts is where Satan wants to keep us. He does not want us to understand everything we get when we get His Name!

"I will set him on high because he has known my Name."

The Shulamite lady is us, courted by the Lord God Himself, but well-aware of her darkness, her sin nature. How could such a wonderful God desire me? How can I ever live up to His expectations? Can this be real? Dare I take God at His word and chase after Him? Can I really say, Yes?

Yes! That is exactly what God is saying, dare to chase me while I am love drunk over you! Draw near to Me and I will draw even nearer to you! Allow Me to cleanse you in My blood and you will be whiter than snow, and we can dance in the high places together! The high places of who I have called and gifted you to be. I know your design better than you yourself, for I am the One who designed you. Let Me show you what I put in you, and who you are meant to be.

Folks, this is literally a dream come true. The American dream? It doesn't hold a candle compared to God's Sky Kingdom. It will grow old and fade, like rags washed too many times. There is no eternal power in the American Dream, but only a hollowness that never satisfies. All things are possible with God. Nothing is possible without

Him. For without God, we all are nothing but dead-end streets. Our lives are nothing but dead-end streets, and rather short streets at that. As I said, Ecclesiastes prepares us to embrace Song of Songs.

The American Dream use to say, "In God we trust." But no more. That has become a lie printed on paper money we are trying hard to get rid of. "They" will get rid of this soon enough. "They" might as well, it's no longer true anyway.

But if by some miracle it could be true again? It is a fearful thing that the prayer of Elijah might be the only prayer that could cause such a revival. God knows those of His people who embrace the wisdom of all three of Solomon's Books.

CHAPTER SEVEN

"Look! Listen! There's my lover! Do you see him coming? Vaulting the mountains, leaping the hills. My lover is like a gazelle, graceful; like a young stag, virile. Look at him there, on tiptoe at the gate, all ears, all eyes – ready! My lover has arrived and he's speaking to me!"

— Song of Songs 2: 8-10 (Message Bible)

He's speaking to me? I wonder if that's how Zacheus felt? When our Lord spotted him in the high place, in the tree he had climbed "up" into, and Jesus called him to Himself. Wow. He's speaking to me?!

What is this call to the high places of God? Everyone should have a vision for their life. And as visions are achieved, new visions come. We are created to be a visionary people in the image of God. So, let's imagine for a moment, God has not been a part of your big picture about life. And now you're considering if it could be possible that there is a God, He has given a book full of the details, and He is offering us to become His spiritual

Bride in which we gain His Name and everything that goes with it? Could this really be true?

Wow... that would be a game-changer, would it not? If we compared this life to a game, that would bring major changes to how we play the game. For one thing, we would know the Book God has given is priceless, because it's got all the test answers, all the code keys, everything we need to know as to how this game is designed, how it works, and how it can be worked to our favor. The keys to winning the game.

Now let's say the person who has made you aware of all this, chose to describe it to you not as just "getting-saved", but as the act of saying "yes" to Jesus asking you to marry Him. Woe! This description alone should immediately give you some idea of what you're considering doing. We all have some understanding of what marriage is, what it means, and how it works.

On the one hand you have the opportunity of a lifetime to gain everything in the Name of the One you would be joining. However, on the other hand, you might be asking yourself, what does it mean to be "one" with God? We will be living in the same house, together. I can't just ignore God anymore. And what does that mean? How do I learn to live in a proper way with God? How do we share this house together forever?

Also, He's the male figure in this picture. I'm the female. He will listen to me because He loves me greatly, but if push comes to shove, if I'm wrong about something, He is the head of our household. He gets the final say and I'm supposed to say, "Yes, Sir. I know your wisdom is always right. You are protecting me from harm."

But even if I fail to say, "Yes, Sir." If, in my stubbornness I choose my way. He will still love me. At some point I will have to come back and be reconciled to Him. We can't live in the same house and just ignore each other. I can't just think about myself and my desires anymore. I've got to also consider the desires of the One I claim to love, and I married.

And there's that word again, love. Do I love Him? Because if I do, it is love that will bring me back around. God created us as beings who are moved by what or who we love. We are made in the image of God, and God is love. John chapter three says:

> *"And this is the condemnation, that the light has come into the world, **and men loved darkness rather than light**, because their deeds were evil. For everyone practicing evil hates the light, and does not come to the light, lest his deeds should be exposed. But he who does the truth comes to the light, that his deeds may be clearly seen, that they have been done in God." — John 3:19-21 (NKJ)*

God's wisdom in basing it all on love, is amazing. And now we also understand, when the Bible says God is love, it's not joking. God created this whole creation to work according to the laws of love, not the laws of Commandments. He wanted us to see the difference. The law needed to come first, so we could understand how much higher and better the ways of His love are.

We also needed to understand what sin is. What is right and wrong, good and evil, light and darkness. The Commandments and the law do a good job of revealing and educating us in these matters. The law needed to come first, like a schoolteacher teaching us we are guilty, and we would know God's love is NOT a license to sin.

The spiritual law of reaping what we sow still applies. As much as God wants to protect us, many times reaping what we have sown is the only thing that wakes us up to realizing that loving God is so much better. At that point, God can begin to fix us again, get us back on the right track, and fix our mess.

Often, fear is the "beginning" of our wisdom, but God constantly calls us to the high places of His love. (America is reaping what she has sown. We need repentance, forgiveness, a change of direction, and a crop failure! Because we have sown a lot of bad. How large could this dark crop be? The prayer of Elijah?)

So, He calls us to these high places and we need the feet of the gazelle to live there. It is as if we are cripples that need our feet healed before we can even begin answering His call. He delivers us from Egypt and takes us into the wilderness. He begins healing our feet and offering us the wings of the eagle, if we will only learn His Promised Land ways. Or we wander in the wilderness our whole life, still having crippled feet. He takes care of us even there, but He offers us so much more!

A wonderful book that was written by a lady named Hannah Hurnard, called, *Hind's Feet in High Places,* has always been a favorite of mine. The allegory she wrote is much like what I'm describing in this book.

Marriage is a devotion between two people who separate themself to each other. The bed is not defiled when it is in holy matrimony. Two people faithful to each other, and they go to bed with none other, they live with none other, their marriage to each other comes first no matter what.

The integrity of the marriage is of utmost importance. They are there for each other, for better or for worse. And they know they can count on each other. They will defend each other against any foe. They are devoted to the marriage. They are one. No one comes between them. Love has done this.

When I think of the life that is in biblical love. When I remember falling in love with my wife. I look back on that madness of passion, and there is nothing like it. And now I see five people who were created and born out of the love we had for each other. All five were created from the love we had for each other. And now they too have love children. Eleven grandchildren have been born to us, and how many births will come from them?

I am amazed at what the love between two people can produce. Love, not fear. My wife and I have created something that continues growing and multiplying. When we are both gone, the life of our love will still be affecting this earth. Our name is carried on. And it should be so in our marriage to Christ also. New births because of our own love and relationship to Jesus our Husband. The Name of Christ carried on. How many children might be born, and how great the potential effect?

But now we shall begin looking at the challenge of a good marriage, because we have an enemy in our flesh who wants to destroy our love. There will be good times and there will be bad. But no matter how many times a marriage may get knocked down, a good marriage hangs on, and always eventually gets back up! Especially when God is in the marriage.

From Song of Songs chapter three, verses one through five, here is an example of the good times, and we will follow it with an example of the bad:

> *"Restless in bed and sleepless through the night, I longed for my lover. I wanted him desperately. His absence was painful. So I got up, went out and roved the city, hunting through streets and down alleys. I wanted my lover in the worst way! I looked high and low, and didn't find him."*

> *"And then the night watchmen found me as they patrolled the darkened city. Have you seen my dear lost love? I asked. No sooner had I left them than I found him, found my dear lost love."*

> *"I threw my arms around him and held him tight, wouldn't let him go until I had him home again, safe at home beside the fire. Oh, let me warn you, sisters in Jerusalem, by the gazelles, yes, by all the wild deer: Don't excite love, don't stir it up, until the time is ripe — and you're ready."*

My personal opinion is, that last reference to the sisters of Jerusalem, is a reference to the Jewish nation who will have a turning to Christ in the last days, but do not do it before the appointed time, because it will be a tumultuous time upon the earth, and a very hard time to endure. They will need to be ready.

Other than that, this is the Shulamite again, longing for her lover. Like the deer panting for the water brooks of her soul, a fire is burning in her for her Lord. This is the place to live with Christ, in the flame of our first love.

This fire will not let her sleep. Her lover is drawing her to Himself. She finally rises from her bed, she can't take it anymore, it drives her out into the dark city streets looking for Him. She searches alley ways and dark streets. Love is making her desperate. She is risking all. Do not stir this up, sisters of Jerusalem, until you are ready! It will drive you crazy at times! Unless you are ready.

Finally, the night watchmen find her. She pleads with them, have you seen my Lover? Did they direct her? She finds Him immediately after leaving them. There is a passionate embracing. And she takes Him home to her house and her fire. This is a good night in the relationship.

But we are not perfect. There will also be nights when we fail to rise to our Lover's call. He is always calling us for a reason. We do not know what He might be preparing us against, and what charging of our armor we may be in need of.

He only has our best in mind, but when we, in the weakness of our flesh fail to rise to the occasion, the marriage may suffer for a time. We may be headed for some very troubled waters, but even the storm is for our good, because it will wake us up and drive us back to Him. It will remind us of what is actually important in this fragile life we are living. We now jump to chapter five, starting in verse two.

> *"I was sound asleep, but in my dreams I was wide awake. Oh, listen! It's the sound of my lover knocking, calling!"*

> *"Let me in, dear companion, dearest friend, my dove, consummate lover! I'm soaked with the dampness of the night, drenched with dew, shivering and cold."*

Note: Where has the hardness of heart you are about to see come from? Do you remember the last time you may have been wet, shivering and cold in the night, and in need of comfort, shelter, and heat? How is it that the one she has shown such incredible love for, she is now ready to leave out in the cold? Her own inconvenience causes her to leave Him in the cold? Ahh, but is this not exactly who we are? How does God love us? Our drama continues.

> *"But I'm in my nightgown – do you expect me to get dressed? I'm bathed and in bed – do you want me to get dirty?"*

"But my lover wouldn't take no for an answer, and the longer he knocked, the more excited I became. I got up to open the door to my lover, sweetly ready to receive him, desiring and expectant as I turned the door handle. But when I opened the door he was gone. My loved one had tired of waiting and left."

Note: In the King James version, it also details when she grabbed the door handle...

"I rose to open for my beloved, and my hands dripped with myrrh, my fingers with liquid myrrh, on the handles of the lock."

Myrrh was used as an ingredient in the holy anointing oil for consecrating priests, the tabernacle, and kings. It also was used for embalming bodies, foreshadowing Christ's own death on the cross. Its name represented a bitter taste.

At this point, our Shulamite lady is about to go through some very hard things, but she is willing to pay a price. She knows she has hurt the one she loves. She's willing to do anything to say I'm sorry, I need you, please forgive and restore me to our high places together.

We all miss it sometimes. How quick are we to make it right when we do? If our love is true, we will not wait long. But if we have something less than true love, it is revealed in our actions if we really care or not, if Christ is important, or not? Perhaps it even indicates if we're really married, or not. The drama continues:

> *"And I died inside – oh, I felt so bad! I ran out looking for him, but he was nowhere to be found. I called into the darkness – but no answer came. The night watchmen found me as they patrolled the streets of the city. They slapped and beat and bruised me, ripping off my clothes, these watchmen, who were supposed to be guarding the city."*

> *"I beg you, sisters in Jerusalem — if you find my lover, please tell him I want him, that I'm heartsick with love for him."*

Absence should make the heart grow fonder if it is love. Our Shulamite is afire with passion again, and she is asking for help. Evidently, she was made to wait for a time. He is king, we are not. And sometimes we only learn through hard lessons, like the Elijah prayer. The Watchmen who were nice to her before, now beat her. These can be very difficult lessons, but if we are sincere…

> *"So where has this love of yours gone, fair one? Where on earth can he be? Can we help you look for him?"*

77

"Never mind. My lover is already on his way to his garden, to browse among the flowers, touching the colors and forms. I am my lover's and my lover is mine. He caresses the sweet-smelling flowers."

It seems she has been up all night searching for him, and now they will reunite in a place of His choosing, and He has chosen a flower garden, a type of garden of Eden perhaps.

Song of Songs is a rich romance with One who dances upon the mountains and calls His Bride to do the same, to seek those things which are above, fall in love with those things rather than this world.

CHAPTER EIGHT

We have spoken of love being stronger than fear. The Old Covenant was fear based with its emphasis on the Ten Commands. Thou shalt not! Thou shalt! And if we reject the love God is offering in Christ Jesus, we reveal we love darkness, and we will face the God of the Ten Commands on judgement day. Those commands are still legally valid for the unforgiven, those who reject light to love darkness. All of God's commands are commands of love, for the good of all. Only lovers of darkness would reject them.

God is offering us love. The angels marvel over what God is offering man. Consider the words of the Psalmist in Chapter eight, (KJV):

> *"What is man that you are mindful of him, the son of man that you care for him? You made him a little lower than the heavenly beings and crowned him with glory and honor."*

Consider Chapter eight, verses 3-9 (Message Bible):

"I look up at your macro-skies, dark and enormous, your handmade sky-jewelry, moon and stars mounted in their settings. Then I look at my micro-self and wonder, why do you bother with us? Why take a second look our way?"

"Yet we've so narrowly missed being gods, bright with Eden's dawn light. You put us in charge of your handcrafted world, made us stewards of sheep and cattle, even animals out in the wild, birds flying and fish swimming, whales singing in the ocean deeps."

"God, brilliant Lord, your name echoes around the world."

"And did he (God) ever say anything like this to an angel? Sit alongside me here on my throne until I make your enemies a stool for your feet. Isn't it obvious that all angels are sent to help out with those lined up to receive salvation?"

— Hebrews 1: 13-14

What is man that you are mindful of him? We will judge angels? First Corinthians 6: 2-3 (Message Bible):

"The day is coming when the world is going to stand before a jury made up of followers of Jesus. If someday you are going to rule on the world's fate, wouldn't it be a good idea to prac-

*tice on some of these smaller cases? Why, we're
even going to judge angels!"*

God's word reveals God to be a "relationship" God, and we are made in His image, so declares God's word. That is such an important point that it is declared right at the beginning of our whole story! This is man's story, not some aliens from outer space. And the real story is so much better than the fictional!

God has just finished creating the earth and all its creatures except man. And it says He created the animals "after their kind", and plants "after their kind". But then there is like this holy pause, and you can feel a drum roll building, as God says: *Let us make man in OUR image.* (And I think the angels said, "Do what?!" Shock and awe!)

> *"God spoke: Let us make human beings in our image, make them reflecting our nature so they can be responsible for the fish in the sea, the birds in the air, the cattle, and, yes, Earth itself, and every animal that moves on the face of Earth."*
>
> *"God created human beings; he created them godlike, reflecting God's nature. He created them male and female."*
>
> — Genesis 1: 26-27 (Message Bible)

81

The Bible is a romance adventure. It begins with a marriage when God creates Adam and Eve and declares them to be one. And then, thousands of years later, after such a great Hero's Journey, the Bible ends with a great wedding in Heaven, the Marriage Feast of the Lamb (Jesus), and the Bride (us).

We are made in God's image and nature, and God creates according to specified relationships. The angels do not have the same relationship to God as we do, and they marvel at our opportunity. No angel has ever been asked to sit alongside God on the throne of all thrones.

And yet, I am sure angels are "fulfilled" in living what they are created to be. An angel finds great meaning, purpose, and passion in being what God created them to be. Nothing else will satisfy them to their core being than their God-designed purpose. God has gifted and equipped them to do exactly what they do.

Animals also have a different relationship. Jesus rode a donkey into Jerusalem. God had a whale swallow Jonah and deliver him where he was supposed to be. He had ravens feed Elijah. When God created animals, He had a certain relationship in mind. And when God creates, He builds into the creation a desire for their purpose and calling. We are fulfilled when we live in harmony with our God-given design. Just as it is in the nature of a fish to be a fish.

Do we, as humans do the same thing as God when we create? Do we create with a certain relationship in mind? I believe we do. Did the hammer have a certain relationship to us when we created it? And every improvement we've made to it over the years? I believe it does. The relationship we had in mind was to hold it in our hand, swing it, and hit things! Like driving in nails. And to pry on things. Such as pulling nails. It is a building tool or destroying tool.

When we create, if the creation fails to have a useful relationship to us, it goes to the scrap yard. It's back to the drawing board and try again. Mankind has had a wonderful relationship with the automobile. What person does not look forward to when they own and drive their very first car? It's a type of freedom. It is transportation, shelter, comfort, music, and etc. We love our cars.

A muscle car has a certain relationship to us. If it fails to be fast, we are disappointed. A luxury car is a different relationship, and a pickup truck even more different. And there are four-wheel drive vehicles for off-roading. Semis for hauling big loads. Boats, trains, etc. A rocket to fly to the moon in outer space, where there is no oxygen!

It's all about our relationship and purpose for the things we create.

Now consider what your Bible declares the call of man is, to be the Bride of the Lamb, to be higher than angels, to sit on a throne, to rule and reign alongside our Husband in a new earth and new heaven! How much more incredible could it be! But none of it is ours without His Name, because it is inherited by way of a Biblical marriage. It is all for the Lamb's Bride. Wow. And the angels marvel. So should we.

So, let's continue a little longer in Song of Songs and consider a little more about the power of love. Here the Shulamite woman is speaking to her lover:

> *"Hang my locket around your neck, wear my ring on your finger. Love is invincible facing danger and death. Passion laughs at the terrors of hell. The fire of love stops at nothing – it sweeps everything before it. Flood waters can't drown love, torrents of rain can't put it out. Love can't be bought, love can't be sold — it's not to be found in the market place."*

— Song of Songs 8:6-8

Did you notice the part of wearing my ring on your finger? The Shulamite speaks of her ring on His finger. Here on earth at least, a marriage is usually signified by a ring. Every time I think of us being His Bride, I can't help but imagine a Ring going with His Name. It's obvious the Shulamite thinks this way, but we shall see when the great wedding happens on that day. I can hardly wait!

Perhaps we have the engagement Ring at this point. Perhaps we are walking in the power of the engagement Ring. But we need the other part! In heaven, on that day, we will receive the whole wedding Ring! Imagine the power of that day! Blessed are all those who are invited to the Wedding Feast of the Lamb! Just imagine. Try to imagine.

It is so obvious that a relationship of "law" was never what God had in mind for us. Love is so much better, more powerful, and more important than law or fear. God created us for His highest wishes and relationship. Song of Songs makes it plain that love is God's way. David understood it also, even in a time of law. Jesus made it plain also, in His teaching of the two greatest commands that fulfills all law. And Paul was used of God to make it plain in First Corinthians 12, the Love Chapter:

> *"If I speak with human eloquence and angelic ecstasy but don't have love, I'm nothing but the creaking of a rusty gate."*
>
> *"If I speak God's Word with power, revealing all his mysteries and making everything plain as*

> *day, and if I have faith that says to a mountain,*
> *"Jump," and it jumps, but I don't have love, I'm*
> *nothing."*

> *"If I give everything I own to the poor and even*
> *go to the stake to be burned as a martyr, but I*
> *don't love, I've gotten nowhere. So, no matter*
> *what I say, what I believe, and what I do, I'm*
> *bankrupt without love."*

That is an extremely high bar set for love. This is the whole point of our creation, training, and journey with God. If we don't learn this, then we have learned nothing. Law is a danger to love. Be careful with law. Its purpose is to make us aware we are sinners, and we need a Savior. It proves us guilty! And condemned. However, for God so loved the world… God so loved us that He came as our Knight in sacred armor to save His damsel in distress. He came to rescue us from the dragon and woo us to His love.

This chapter goes on to say many powerful things about love, but its' final verse and statement ends this way:

> *"But right now, until that completeness, we*
> *have three things to do to lead us toward that*
> *consummation: Trust steadily in God, hope*

unswervingly, love extravagantly. And the best of the three is love."

Solomon could take his writings no further because he had reached the highest level. There was no higher place to go. Paul would not write what Solomon knew for many, many years yet, but when he did, it confirms every word of Song of Songs.

Song of Songs ends with these words:

> *The Male Figure says: "King Solomon may have vast vineyards in lush, fertile country, where he hires others to work the ground. People pay anything to get in on that bounty. But my vineyard is all mine, and I'm keeping it to myself. You can have your vast vineyards, Solomon, you and your greedy guests!"*
>
> *"Oh, lady of the gardens, my friends are with me listening. Let me hear your voice!"*
>
> *The Female Figure says: "Run to me, dear lover. Come like a gazelle, leap like a wild stag on the spice mountains."*

I point out here that the male refers to his lover as the "lady of the gardens." If you remember in chapter one, she was ashamed of her dark skin because she had been made to work the fields, and care for the face of the earth, but had no time to care for her own face.

I like to think that her caring for the face of the earth had developed her skills in gardening, and that which she thought would bring her shame, had now become a point of great benefit between her and her lover. I believe her lover had led her to the mountains of spiritual spices in which she thrived in her fulfillment of who she was called to be, with Him. What a happy ending! And it is to be our ending! Praise our God forever!

CHAPTER NINE

There is a movement developing in which they are teaching "we are Gods." I want to slay that teaching right now! It needs to be thrown into the pit of hell! There is a big difference between Jesus saying, "we are gods," and man saying, "we are Gods." That big "G" and little "g" is a major difference. And I believe this illustration of "the Bride" is a great way to understand the difference. Again, the analogy holds so perfectly true.

Jesus teaches that through this spiritual rebirth of being born-again, we become one with Him, but that does not make us "Him" any more than my wife has become "me". We still have our differences. In the eyes of God, we are one in a way like Adam and Eve were one. God referred to them both as Adam. She was eventually given the name, Eve.

As the "Bride" and the "female", we have our role to play. It is not the same as the position Jesus, as the male, plays. We have become one, but He is still the head! We are the body. My body tries to do what my brain tells it to. It may fail, but it always wants to. If we were a big "G" God, then we would not need to obey and follow someone who is over us.

This big "G" false teaching is very dangerous. They may even claim that is not what they are teaching, but they have to know it is the way it comes across. I want to make sure people do not make this little book as part of that teaching. I boldly declare there is a difference between the King and His wife, the Queen! And the illustration itself should be without question that it shows such a difference.

A big "G" God is King, and answers to no one. However, scripture makes it plain that we are not the head, and we answer to the head. There can be no disputing these scriptural facts. It is also plain that we have a very high position, even above the angels, and we need to know that. Satan is meant to be under our feet. But God is still God, and we are NOT. End of discussion. I'm still a created being. God is not, and He is the only One who is not.

The Godhead is certainly a great mystery to us, even as the Apostle Paul declared. I'm sure in being the Bride of the Lamb it will all be made plain in its proper time. Until then, we walk by faith, and we do not let pride go to our head and think we are more than we are. The creation can never claim to be the Creator. That would be something akin to the mind of Satan.

We now begin winding down this little book. I felt from the beginning keeping this book smaller for easy reading would be best. So, we will share a few more things as we lean towards a final page. I cannot help but think of the Apostle John in all this, who had the great vision of the Marriage Feast and the Bride. He was the one who leaned his head on the Lord's shoulder at that final meal. He was also the only disciple to live well into old age before passing. John begins his book with:

> *"The Word was first, the Word present to God, God present to the Word. The Word was God, in readiness for God from day one."*

> *"Everything was created through him; nothing — not one thing! — came into being without him. What came into existence was Life, and the Life was Light to live by. The Life – Light blazed out of the darkness; the darkness couldn't put it out."*   — John 1:1-5

> *"The Life — Light was the real thing: every person entering Life he brings into Light. He was in the world, the world was there through him, and yet the world didn't even notice. He came to his own people, but they didn't want him. But whoever did want him, who believed*

he was who he claimed and would do what he said, he made to be their true selves, their child-of-God selves. These are the God-begotten, not blood-begotten, not flesh-begotten, not sex-begotten."

"The Word became flesh and blood, and moved into the neighborhood. We saw the glory with our own eyes, the one-of-a-kind glory, like Father, like Son, generous inside and out, true from start to finish." — VRS 9-14

Who could write such a story? And yet, this is OUR story. Not just a story we read, but we can choose to live! Yes, we have entered into a type of godhood through Christ, but how long does it take for us to learn how it works? How much have we mastered and how much have we not? How much have we not even begun to comprehend? And how many of us might even be completely off track, and needing to make a course correction as new revelation, new light, enters our understanding?

According to scripture, as a true believer we have become the God-begotten. The very thought of that amazes me. Even the angels stand in awe and wonder. That transformation was made "possible" through Christ Jesus, our Savior, our Knight, as He paid the extremely high price that was on our heads. It was made "possible" by His death, burial, and resurrection. It was made "possible" by the power of His righteous blood cleansing us from our sins. It was made "possible"… but it only actually becomes "ours" when we enter into a very special Covenant relationship in which we receive His Name! That relationship is symbolically compared to a marriage, in which we have said "Yes" to marrying God!

Biblical marriage is a type of picture of what God is expecting in this relationship. It is one of the reasons we must say "Yes" if we desire to enter it. We do not force someone we love to marry us. The potential husband asks the woman if she will marry him. If she says "No", and will not change her mind, then the man will not force her. It is not the kind of relationship he wants. And he loves her too much to force a marriage against her own will.

Scripture clearly explains the salvation dilemma we face. Our flesh is attracted to sin. In our sin-nature we have an attraction to sin, a love affair with sin. Many people refuse to say "Yes" to Christ because He is Light and they love darkness. Their love for darkness is overpowering for them. A part of them actually hates the Light and loves darkness.

But for all those who love the Light even in spite of their lust for darkness, and they cry out to God, "Lord save me from my own darkness!" If their heart is true, God hears their cry and will save them. His work in them begins, and the battle to crucify our flesh and please the One we love begins.

No one says it will be easy, but it leads to the most meaningful and eternal life a mortal can ever have. God-begotten into a marriage with the Son-of-God Himself. It is a Spirit relationship built on Spirit laws and principals. It is the same and yet different than what we experience in the flesh.

Even the Apostle Paul spoke of this:

> *"No one abuses his own body, does he? No, he feeds and pampers it. That's how Christ treats us, the church, since we are part of his body. And this is why a man leaves father and mother and cherishes his wife. No longer two, they become "one flesh." <u>This is a huge mystery, and I don't pretend to understand it all.</u> What is clearest to me is the way Christ treats the church. And this provides a good picture of how each husband is to treat his wife, loving himself in loving her, and how each wife is to honor her husband."*
>
> — Ephesians 5:29-33 (Message Bible)

Even the Apostle Paul said it was a huge mystery. But it is the Gospel message! Peace on earth! Good-will towards man! Made possible by this incredible mystery! It is God's offer to us if we have the faith to believe and accept! At which point the rest of our life becomes a journey of honoring this spiritual marriage we have entered in with Christ.

How simple can it be, really? Has God asked something of us we cannot understand? No, He has not. What does it mean to honor your husband, and honor your vow of marriage? As we are drawing closer to the finish line of this book, we would be remiss if we did not consider the book of Hosea. If the book of Song of Songs were one part of a pair of bookends, perhaps Hosea would be the other part. Let's go there now and see what we can glean from its' revelations about this God, our Creator, we are trying to understand.

If we fail to honor the marriage and honor our Husband, how does God view it? What does God compare it to? Once again, God's past-history with the nation Israel becomes our greatest teacher. A clue might be found in Matthew 19: 3-8 Message Bible. We will pick up in those scriptures in chapter ten.

CHAPTER TEN

One day the Pharisees were badgering him (Jesus): "Is it legal for a man to divorce his wife for any reason?"

He answered, "Haven't you read in your Bible that the Creator originally made man and woman for each other, male and female? And because of this, a man leaves father and mother and is firmly bonded to his wife — no longer two bodies but one. Because God created this organic union of the two sexes, no one should desecrate his art by cutting them apart."

They shot back in rebuttal, "If that's so, why did Moses give instructions for divorce papers and divorce procedures?"

Jesus said, "Moses provided for divorce as a concession to your hard heartedness, but it is not part of God's original plan."

— Matthew 19: 3-8 (Message Bible)

Some Church denominations believe "once-saved-always-saved". In other words, there is no divorce with God. If we have been born-again, we cannot lose our salvation, but we might sin-unto-death. These are deep subjects of which whole denominations differ as to what is true. However, I can say with assurance, if we can lose our salvation, it does not happen easily. I think this is where the book of Hosea sheds a lot of light.

Hosea could be considered a tragic love story. The story begins in a highly unusual way when a man of God, called to be a prophet, hears God speak to him for the very first time! And what he hears would blow the mind of any normal person, and that is: *"I want you to go and marry a harlot!"* Why might God ask such a thing of one of His prophets?

Yes, why indeed? Israel were the "people of God" at that time. They were supposed to be "set apart", separated to God as a holy nation. They were supposed to be evangelizing the world with God's message. But instead, and at this particular time, they had fallen into much idolatry and worshipping of false gods/ idols. They were backslidden in sin, worshipping idols, completely unfaithful to the one true God, and headed towards heavy judgement if they did not change direction.

God instructed Hosea, His prophet, to marry a prostitute as a living picture to the people of what they were doing spiritually. The nation had become prostitutes whoring after other gods and pleasures. But they were supposed to be separated to God. They were failing miserably. What is going to happen?

> *"All things are lawful for me, but all things are not helpful. All things are lawful for me, but I will not be brought under the power of any. Foods for the stomach and the stomach for foods, but God will destroy both it and them. Now the body is not for sexual immorality but for the Lord, and the Lord for the body. And God both raised up the Lord and will also raise us up by His power."*

> *"Do you not know that your bodies are members of Christ? Shall I then take the members of Christ and make them members of a harlot? Certainly not! Or do you not know that he who is joined to a harlot is one body with her? For "the two," He says, "shall become one flesh. But he who is joined to the Lord is one spirit with Him."*

> *"Flee sexual immorality. Every sin that a man does is outside the body, but he who commits sexual immorality sins against his own body. Or do you not know that your body is the temple of the Holy Spirit who is in you, whom*

you have from God, and you are not your
own?" (Again, like a marriage. I now belong
to another.)

"For you were bought at a price; therefore glo-
rify God in your body and in your spirit, which
are God's." — 1st Corinthians 6:12-20 (NKJ)

Don't forget God had to "purchase" us for a price. A very high price. We were sold into the slavery of sin by the fall of Adam and Eve. We were already under a different ownership. An ownership of death and destruction. We had no way out.

We could never pay our own price for our freedom. Perfection was a price we were no longer capable of paying. Neither could we raise from the dead! In other words, there was no light at the end of our tunnel. But God became that light, and he always was, and always will be.

But God could not simply "steal" us back. That would be sin. God had to legally "buy" us back, and so He did. We were bought with a price. We are literally His possession by way of creation, and He also purchased us back when we were lost from Him. An interesting thought I just had; our marriage makes like a trinity of ownership of us. Not sure if that means anything, but it is a cool thought.

When we become a Christian, we are separated to God. We are espoused to Christ. Perhaps a spiritual engagement Ring is slid on our finger. But we are capable of being unfaithful to the Covenant we entered, and what happens then? What does it compare to?

It compares to us committing spiritual adultery. We play the harlot, cheating on God. It causes our Husband great pain, grieving the Holy Spirit within us. God has every right to divorce us, but is that what He wants to do? Obviously, according to Jesus, it is not. Divorce was never God's desire for us.

Herein lies where "fear" should enter in. We should fear "tempting" God by playing the harlot and going whoring after the things of this earth. In the case of Israel, great judgement did eventually fall on them. They were taken captive to Babylon and forced into slavery, which is what sin does to us. It is a type of slavery.

Some people will eventually repent and change once judgement falls on them, which is what Israel eventually did. So, this story has a happy ending even though it suffers much tragedy along the way. But what about the person who refuses to repent even while in judgement? They continue whoring themselves after other gods and idols. That is the question many denominations continue debating. Personally, I do not recommend testing God's grace to such a degree. Personally, I would be very afraid of that. This is where fear would be highly recommended as the beginning of wisdom and getting back right with God!

I spent many years as a truck driver. I did a lot of running at nighttime. One night I was covering another man's route while he was off. As I was unloading the delivery from the trailer, a woman came out of nowhere and asked if she could "please me"! Her offer was plainly understood. I was taken totally by surprise.

The only thing I could think of to say to her was, "Lady, have you no fear of God?"

Now she was taken aback. I don't think she expected such a question. LOL. She finally shot back with, "Well, the other guy does it!"

I answered, "I guess I'm not that guy."

As she walked away, I heard her say, "A woman's got to survive somehow."

How ever we may rationalize why we dishonor our Covenant to Christ in our own mind, it's still wrong! God sees our heart and he knows when we hate something, and we're wrestling with it, but we may have failures. God always sees truth no matter what excuses we may make. He knows when we embrace something, because we love it, and make no effort to change.

Hosea's wife, whose name is Gomer, already had a past-history of being a prostitute. She knew what that lifestyle offered. She knew both the good, bad, and ugly of it. It was familiar ground for her. We also know what a life of sin has to offer. We were born sinners. We know the good, bad, and ugly of it before we came to Christ.

Sinning does have its' pleasures. All of it very short lived and over-priced. We are all capable of falling to temptation, becoming a prodigal son/daughter. We understand what the story of Hosea is showing us. You might be there right now, struggling with a sin that so easily besets you. What do we learn from the story of Hosea and Gomer?

The Apostle Paul told us God's grace is not a license to sin. The prodigal son was fortunate that he lived long enough to have a change of heart and come back home to his father. That was the story of the prodigal son who decided he did not like the pig pen once all his money had run out. That was the judgement God allowed to fall in hopes of him coming to his senses before it was too late. But let's check a few highlights from Hosea's and Gomer's story.

> *"The first time God spoke to Hosea he said:*
> *Find a whore and marry her. Make this whore*
> *the mother of your children. And here's why:*

This whole country has become a whorehouse, unfaithful to me, God."

"Hosea did it. He picked Gomer daughter of Diblaim. She got pregnant and gave him a son."

"Then God told him: Name him Jezreel. It won't be long now before I'll make the people of Israel pay for the massacre at Jezreel. I'm calling it quits on the kingdom of Israel. Payday is coming! I'm going to chop Israel's bows and arrows into kindling in the valley of Jezreel."

"Gomer got pregnant again. This time she had a daughter. God told Hosea: Name this one No-Mercy. I'm fed up with Israel. I've run out of mercy. There's no more forgiveness."

— Book of Hosea, chapter one,
starting verse two (Message Bible)

I think we get the idea. After this daughter, she had another son who was named, Nobody.

"Name him Nobody. You've become nobodies to me, and I, God, am a nobody to you."

If there is one Being you should never want to be a "nobody" to, it is God. But this is where sin takes us. We become more and more dead inside. Satan comes to steal, kill, and destroy. He has no other agenda. As we play with sin, we are in great danger of going spiritually numb, no longer feeling a desire or passion for God. We have become dead inside. God becomes a nobody to us. Our conscience burned out, unable to feel, unable to set off the alarm of the great danger we are in.

At the end of chapter one and beginning chapter two, God begins to prophesy the change that will come to Israel, and He says you will rename your brothers as "God's Somebody". And rename your sister as "All Mercy". This is the plan of God even when He is correcting us. But will we respond? It's still our choice.

In chapter two, verses 14-15, God's Word says:

> *"And now, here's what I'm going to do: I'm going to start all over again. I'm taking her back out into the wilderness where we had our first date, and I'll court her. I'll give her bouquets of roses. I'll turn Heartbreak Valley into Acres of Hope. She'll respond like she did as a young girl, those days when she was fresh out of Egypt."*

God offers us the Promised Land, but if we need more wilderness time, He can do that too. Notice how this all sounds like a typical dating and wooing process leading towards a hopeful marriage. This is how God sees our relationship. The whole Bible is one incredible romance for all those who say, "Yes". And those who say, No? Well... sad to say, they remain a part of the dragon who gets sentenced to the second death. If you don't want to end up there, don't be in league with the dragon. God Himself, our Lord, will personally defeat the dragon. Indeed, already has! Satan does not want you to enter God's victory for us.

But some of us stay in that wilderness, just like the Children of Israel did. The generation who came out of Egypt died in the wilderness, except for two. Only two had a different heart and God kept them and brought them into the Promised Land with the younger generation.

If we are faithful, as a marriage vow calls for, God will lead us through the growing pains of the wilderness and bring us into an abundant life flowing with milk and honey. We will know the joy and power of His salvation. He will turn our water to wine. He will do the heavy lifting for His Bride. He will give us the feet of the gazelle to leap in our high places.

During these first two chapters God is speaking about the nation Israel, not Gomer, but it appears during that time Gomer must have gone back to her whoring ways too, even as Israel was doing. Because in chapter three we find a most amazing twist to the plot we have been reading to this time.

> "Then God ordered me, Start all over: Love your wife again, your wife who is in bed with her latest boyfriend, your cheating wife."

> "Love her the way I, God, love the Israelite people, even as they flirt and party with every god that takes their fancy."

> "I did it. I paid good money to get her back. It cost me the price of a slave."

> "Then I told her, from now on you're living with me. No more whoring, no more sleeping around. You're living with me and I'm living with you."

God sees us in a marriage, and we have the story of Hosea and Gomer to have some idea just how much God loves us and to the great extent He will go for our salvation. But is there an eventual limit? That is the question denominations have wrestled with for a solid answer. This story would seem to say there is no limit. It would "seem" to indicate that, but we can't be sure, and I could show other scriptures that "seem" to say the other way. This book is not about solving that riddle, even if I could.

What we do know is God loves us greatly and will not easily let go. We're not going to "accidentally" lose our salvation. We will walk on the blood of Christ the whole way to our judgement, if that be the case. It is God's desire for all to be saved, but we must still say, "Yes". We must say, "NO" to the dragon, and "YES" to God's Knight, Jesus Christ. Here's some more interesting scriptures, starting in chapter five, the last verse; and the first three verses of chapter six.

> *(God is speaking.) "No one can help them. Then I'll go back to where I came from until they come to their senses. When they finally hit rock bottom, maybe they'll come looking for me."*

> *(People speaking.) "Come on, let's go back to God. He hurt us, but he'll heal us. He hit us hard, but he'll put us right again. In a couple days we'll feel better. By the third day he'll have made us brand-new, alive and on our feet, fit to face him. We're ready to study God, eager for God-knowledge. As sure as dawn breaks, so sure is his daily arrival. He comes as rain comes, as spring rain refreshing the ground."*

These are people coming to their senses. These people have an understanding of what has been happening, and what needs to be done to fix everything. They can personally make the right choices and see the change in their personal life, but will the whole nation turn around? Are enough of the people understanding and ready to change? This is the dilemma we live in. Even in America, who has seen such high places with God in her past, but now only seems to have eyes for the pleasures of this world. Consider these scriptures at the beginning of chapter nine:

> *(God speaking.) "Don't waste your life in wild orgies, Israel. Don't party away your life with the heathen. You walk away from your God at the drop of a hat and like a whore sell yourself promiscuously at every sex-and-religion party on the street. All that party food won't fill you up. You'll end up hungrier than ever. At this rate you'll not last long in God's land: Some of you are going to end up bankrupt in Egypt. Some of you will be disillusioned in Assyria."*

> *"As refugees in Egypt and Assyria, you won't have much chance to worship God – Sentenced to rations of bread and water, and your souls polluted by the spirit-dirty air. You'll be starved for God, exiled from God's own country."*

In the last chapter of Hosea, chapter fourteen, the book ends with God still calling Israel back to Himself. The first verse reads: "O Israel, come back! Return to your God! You're down but you're not out. Prepare your confession and come back to God."

This is the God we serve and love. This is the God I desire to marry and be as faithful as I can be all my life.

But even when I fail, He's there, calling me back to Himself. But again, only I can say, "Yes."

CHAPTER ELEVEN

What is beautiful to our Lord, our Husband? This should be our main concern. What is the main concern of every wife in a marriage? Is she concerned about being stronger than her husband? Is that what she desires? Is she lying awake at night worried about not being stronger than her husband? Surely not. That would be ludicrous. Why set yourself up for failure?

Is a four-cylinder engine going to outpull a V8? Surely not! "That would be ludicrous!" we shout. It's a matter of design. Of course, the V8 is much stronger than the four. It's not the fault of the four, it is a matter of design.

Is the husband wanting his wife to be stronger than he is? Not likely. That's his department. How embarrassing that would be. So, what is the man looking for in his woman? Her beauty. The many different ways a woman brings beauty into a man's life. And so, we apply this same logic in our marriage to Christ, and what do we see?

What is beautiful in the eyes of God? We know He does not look on the outward, but He looks at the heart.

When God looks at our heart, what does He see? Does He see beauty? Or is there a lot of ugly?

> *"Keep thy heart with all diligence; for out of it are the issues of life."*
>
> — Proverbs 4:23 (KJ)

Keep our heart with all diligence! This is the word of God to us. We need to consider what is beautiful and what is ugly to God? We need to examine our heart, for out of it flows our life. God's word tells us that out of the abundance of our heart, our mouth speaks. It has a huge effect on the sword coming out of our mouth.

When God looks at us, does He see beauty or ugly? If we are His then He will still love us no matter what, but as His Bride, do we not want to be beautiful in His sight? Or are we too busy trying to do His job, i.e. being strong. You see, our strength is in our beauty! You will see that it is the beautiful things God has chosen that end up making us strong by way of a by-product. We become stronger in Him. We get rubbed in His anointing.

However, by the same token, it is the ugly things of life that weaken us. Stink'n think'n weakens us. Sin drains the Holy Spirit from us. A bad mindset, not the mind of Christ, damages us in ways we do not even know. A heart of fear, rather than peace and faith, is not only ugly in God's sight, but allows our enemy power over us he should not have. We need to do a heart check.

How can we have a healthy heart? The mind of Christ is a healthy heart.

> *"Therefore, I urge you, brothers and sisters, in view of God's mercy, to offer your bodies as a living sacrifice, holy and pleasing to God – this is your true and proper worship. Do not conform to the pattern of this world, but be transformed by the renewing of your mind. Then you will be able to test and approve what God's will is – his good, pleasing and perfect will."*
> — Romans 12: 1-2 (NIV)

Be transformed. How? By the renewing of your mind in God's word, the mind of Christ. Worldliness is ugly to God, but we can be transformed! Pride, hate, greed, are all ugly to God, but we can be transformed! The mind of Christ is beautiful to God.

It's actually very easy to do a quick heart-check on yourself. All it requires is complete honesty. That's all. Or do you find that difficult? If so, you're already revealing an ugly heart. If you can't be honest with yourself and God, who can you be honest with?

So… let's give it a test. When you look inside yourself, your emotions, your desires, your hopes and dreams, whatever occupies your thoughts the most when you're free to think, what comes out of your mouth, what do you see and hear?

Which one of these hearts would be beautiful to God, and which would be ugly? A heart filled with simplicity, faith, contentment, joy, and peace? Or... Stress, anxiousness, fear, lust, concern for money, materialism, and jealousy, desire for things.

Why has God made it so easy for us to do a heart check? Because He loves us and has set fate in our favor. He wants us to know, have knowledge, and be in light. He does not want us ignorant and in darkness. We know what is the beautiful heart to God. All we got to do is be honest in our heart check. We can know quickly how we are doing. Are we spiritually healthy or sick? Are we beautiful to our Lover?

In His beauty we enter a REST. He does the heavy lifting. The Promised Land is meant to be a place of peace and beauty. He enables us to overcome the enemy and enjoy the land of His promises. His promises function in alignment with faith, peace, etc. We must live in these things to know His power. We must be filled with these things. We are married to His word, His promises, His holy Spirit.

Now here is wisdom: Logic fails us here. We keep losing our battles because we think in terms of strength, not beauty. We think we're on an ugly battlefield and we got to fight with power and strength! And we are on an ugly battlefield. We got that much right. But we fight through His strength, not ours! And how does His strength come? When we are beautiful in His sight. When our mind and heart are a beautiful place for our Lord to dwell.

Our beauty is more appealing to others as well. Judging others is not beautiful. Loving others in spite of the ugly is beautiful. This kind of sincerity and beauty affects people in the same way Jesus affected them. He was harder on the religious than anyone else. He called them snakes and vipers, but spoke kindly to the lost.

I see an Enoch people. I hear the Lord saying: *Be at peace. Walk with Me. Stay in faith. Be like Enoch.*

> *"By faith Enoch was translated that he should not see death; and he was not found, because God had translated him: for before his translation he had this testimony, that he pleased God."* — Hebrews 11:5

Enoch was very beautiful in God's sight. He walked with God in the beauty of His peace and righteousness, and God took him. Will Enoch and Elijah be back in the Last Days? Good question. It is very possible. But the point is, both Enoch and Elijah are excellent models for us as we go into these Last Days events. It's a very good time for Samuels, too.

When we think of King David, whom God said he was a man after His own heart, is it because he was a mighty warrior? I think it was because he was such a good shepherd. Our Lord is known as the Good Shepherd. David proved himself to be a good shepherd even before he became the mighty warrior. This is very beautiful in God's sight.

If the Church gets purified in the coming fire, could we achieve one more spiritual comeback? There might be one more comeback in us. As the Church gets back to basics and we learn to REST in Him, could we see a Jehosaphat effect and our enemy begins destroying themselves! It could be possible! As we stand and see the salvation of our Lord! Anything will be possible when we're fully RESTING in Him and living in the beauty of His Word.

God's word speaks of the renewing of our mind to think in a different way, a better way, a higher way than we have ever thought before. Perhaps this little book has given you a different perspective on the Christian walk than you have had before? It is likely you have known you are the Bride of the Lamb, but did you see it as the primary reality of your new life in Christ? Did you go farther in your being born-again to realizing you have married God? Is that now the main prism you view your new life through?

Well… if you have not… now you can. And what difference might that make in how you think? Will we focus more on our beauty now? Or fall right back into the old ways of thinking that have left us extremely mediocre at best? It's our choice. Christ has given us everything we need to dwell in high places, to soar, and rise above the standards of this world's mediocrity to live in His Kingdom, NOW! To bring your FUTURE into your PRESENT. To learn how God really intended for us to live.

We tend to think the path to power is by seeking more power. In God's Kingdom that is the way to less power. If we seek perfect peace we will find power. The way to power is by peace. Pursue peace and find power. Pursue power and find neither! With God, seeking less leads to more. Seeking more leads to less. Our Lord is not materialistic, but He is a giver. He showed us serving is better than reigning. Less of this world's ways and thinking leads to more of God. Thou will keep him in perfect peace whose mind is stayed on thee. Beautiful.

We spoke of Samuel earlier. That young lad was given to the temple in Shiloh and cast into a priesthood that had become very ugly in the eyes of man and God. Eli was old, fat, and going blind, way past his prime. His two sons had become downright wicked! Samuel is kind of like a Cinder-fella (Cinderella) story. He was cast into all kinds of ugliness and yet somehow maintained a beautiful heart that was able to hear God. In spite of all his disadvantages, he became one of the greatest prophets of God and led God's people through a very difficult time. He somehow grew in beauty even while surrounded by ugly.

If we seek to rule, then we are jealous when someone else is lifted-up. If we seek to serve, we are happy for them. If we seek what is beautiful in God's sight, then the power we have will be beautiful. If we focus on beauty, not power, then power will be the by-product of our faith in Christ, which naturally flows in the beautiful soul. Amen.

CHAPTER TWELVE

John (the Baptist) answered, "It's not possi-
ble for a person to succeed – without heaven's
help. You yourselves were there when I made
it public that I was not the Messiah but simply
the one sent ahead of him to get things ready.
The one who gets the bride is, by definition,
the bridegroom. And the bridegroom's friend,
his 'best man' –that's me – in place at his side
__where he can hear every word__, is genuinely
happy. How could he be jealous when he knows
that the wedding is finished and the marriage
is off to a good start?"

"That's why my cup is running over. This is the
assigned moment for him to move into the cen-
ter, while I slip off to the sidelines."

— John 3: 27-30

Jesus is described by John the Baptist as the Bridegroom, and again, that makes us the Bride. When I think
of a wedding, I always picture the moment when the
Groom and Bride exchange rings. Our Lord's Ring is the

Ring above of all rings. I want that Rock in my possession, the Rock of my salvation! His Ring is above them all! Every knee shall bow, and every tongue confess that Jesus is Lord!

John the Baptist prepared the way for the Messiah, he served, and got the wedding off to a good start. He was shouting in the desert, "Make straight the paths of the Lord!" He was like a wild man out there, and the people came to hear and see. He did not follow his dad in the temple as a Levite, because God called him to the wilderness to be a prophet.

Now, over two-thousand years later, the call of the Lord is still going strong, and the Bride of the Lamb is being made ready for her day. Even with everything that has been thrown at Christianity, nothing has stopped it. Not the crucifixion of her Lord. Not the murdering of Christians. Not the attempts to destroy all Bibles from the earth. Nothing has been able to stop the Bride of the Lamb. Persecution only seems to make her stronger, becoming more fiery and pure. She becomes hotter! The holy fire of heaven!

We are sealed in the Holy Spirit, and we possess that Ring. Our Lord's coming draws closer every day, and I'm sure the Spirit of God will send forth types of John the Baptist, Samuel, and Elijah in this END TIME. The world will see a fiery and beautiful Church again. The lukewarm will fall away and only the red-hot love drunk people will still be standing.

We recently had a big eclipse event here in Indiana where I live. This happened even as I have been writing this book. Is it a sign from God? Or a personal note of encouragement for me to keep going in this work? I must say, it did inspire me.

I just happened to be in the path of totality, as they say. People traveled from miles around to be here for those three to four minutes. But for me, cool as the totality was, I couldn't help but be impressed with the "Diamond Ring Effect" that happens just prior to the totality. Because I was pondering all these things and writing this book, I couldn't help but smile as I saw the display in the sky, like a sign from God, of a wedding day coming.

The New City Jerusalem, how shall it all be? It boggles my mind to try and imagine these things, but as more and more of the Bible continues coming true, I can't help but believe it's all true. How could any man write such a Book as this? How could any man make the predictions our Bible makes and see it all coming true?

But make special note, John the Baptist spoke of *"being right at the Lord's side, where he could hear every word."* Was he literally physically right at the Lord's side? Not that I can see. The disciples could make such a claim.

They were privileged to walk with Him and be right at his side, even when He was taken. But John the Baptist was also a type of Elijah. And there are things that we as the Bride, need to understand about the LAST DAYS and Elijah. Here we go…

I cannot prove the theories I'm about to share, but my gut has been telling me for a long time that the second coming of our Lord would have a spirit of Elijah about it, who John the Baptist also had a connection to.

Jesus said:

> "Let me tell you what's going on here: No one in history surpasses John the Baptizer; but in the kingdom he prepared for you, the lowliest person is ahead of him. For a long time now people have tried to force themselves into God's kingdom. But if you read the books of the Prophets and God's Law closely, you will see them culminate in John, teaming up with him in preparing the way for the Messiah of the kingdom. Looked at in this way, John is the 'Elijah' you've all been expecting to arrive and introduce the Messiah."
>
> — Matthew 11: 11-14

Jesus speaks here of the great transition about to take place in which "the Law" is no longer the way to heaven, in which every man fails no matter how hard they try, and we move into the New Covenant of grace through faith in

Christ. This is the ending of one dispensation and beginning of another. This is also the first coming of our Lord.

In the second coming of our Lord, we have very much the same spiritual conditions. Jesus is coming, and then the Thousand Year Millennial Reign, which is a change of dispensation. Would we not see a John the Baptist and Elijah type spirit and anointing again? Consider how the Old Testament ends, its' very last words before four-hundred years of silence.

> *"Count on it: The day is coming, raging like a forest fire. All the arrogant people who do evil things will be burned up like stove wood, burned to a crisp, nothing left but scorched earth and ash — a black day. But for you — sunrise! The sun of righteousness will dawn on those who <u>honor my name,</u> healing radiating from its wings. You will be bursting with energy, like colts frisky and frolicking. And you'll tromp on the wicked. They'll be nothing but ashes under your feet on that Day. God-of-the-Angel-Armies says so."*

> *"Remember and keep the revelation I gave through my servant Moses, the revelation I commanded at Horeb for all Israel, all the rules and procedures for right living."*

> *<u>**"But also look ahead:** I'm sending Elijah the prophet to clear the way for the Big Day of</u>*

<u>God — the decisive Judgement Day!</u> He will convince parents to look after their children and children to look up to their parents. If they refuse, I'll come and put the land under a curse."

I believe we will see a repeat of these things in the LAST DAYS. As we see a repeat of very similar conditions, such as the condition of the Church. Remember, Israel was a type of the Church at that time, and Israel was way off track, priest in love with money and pride, they were being ruled by heathens, the Romans, and they did not even recognize the Messiah when He walked among them. Jesus called them hypocrites many times, and said they were blind.

Revelation also reveals a type of Roman Empire again, during the last days. Rome was ruling over God's people the first time our Lord came, and it would seem a certain repeating of history will be happening again. Bring on John the Baptist!

So, what does this mean for you and I, as the Bride? First of all, live as a proper Bride! Stay close to His side! As John the Baptist did so he could hear "every word" the Groom spoke! And this is the spirit of Elijah also!

Remember Elijah in the cave? After he slew all those prophets of Baal? (Oh, by the way, our society and the

Church is once again emersed in Baal worship, in case you're not aware. Once again, very similar conditions.)

Remember how Jeze"baal" swore to murder him? So, he ran for his life and ended up in a cave, where God was ready to confront him? Yeah, it's all such a great story found in 1st Kings 19:

> "I've been working my heart out for the God-of-the-Angel-Armies," said Elijah. "The people of Israel have abandoned your covenant, destroyed the places of worship, and murdered your prophets: I am the only one left, and now they are trying to kill me."
>
> Then he was told, "Go stand on the mountain at attention before God, God will pass by."
>
> A hurricane wind ripped through the mountains and shattered the rocks before God, but God wasn't to be found in the wind; after the wind an earthquake, but God wasn't in the earthquake; and after the earthquake fire, but God wasn't in the fire; and after the fire a gentle and quiet <u>whisper</u>."
>
> "When Elijah heard the quiet voice..."

As the Bride, we need to know the secrets of God. We need to hear His whispers. John the Baptist heard God's whispers. Elijah also heard God's whispers. I believe the

Apostle John, the beloved, when he leaned on the Lord's shoulder at the last supper, also heard our Lord's whispers. And why do we need to hear the whispers? *"He who dwells in the <u>secret place</u> of the most High, shall abide under the shadow of the Almighty."*

Secrets are whispered. The Bride needs to know the secrets of God, abiding right under His shadow, under His wings, under His arms as He protects His Bride. As the Lord's Bride, He desires to share everything with us. Knowledge is power. This is the calling and the privilege of the Bride. What an honor! And what an exciting life to live!

Elijah was the man who did not pray a prayer of blessing on the people of God, but a curse. No more rain until I say so, he said. Years of drought, famine, and suffering. God answered his prayer. Might we be in such a time again? I will say more on this in the last chapter which is coming soon.

As this chapter ends, desire to hear the still small voice of God, His whispers! If we seek to dwell in His secret place, our steps ordered of the Lord, and our water turned to His wine. We need the supernatural power of God in these last days. We can't be entangled with this world and running around chasing an ungodly dream and expect the power of God. With God, less really becomes more. But are we willing to pay such a price?

The prayer of Elijah? Should we also pray such a prayer? Remember how the Old Testament ended with God warning the people if the hearts of the children did not turn to the parents, and their parents to the children, then He would strike the earth with a curse? A hard thing to consider. Are we there?

Can the average American, addicted to such selfishness and luxury really make such sacrifices? Are we willing to pray to be cursed, that we might be powerfully anointed again one day? This will be chapter fourteen, but first, chapter thirteen. We will need chapter thirteen in order to cope better with chapter fourteen.

The next chapter is another very special analogy I love sharing with people. I'm connecting this chapter and illustration to this book because I believe it belongs here. It adds another way of understanding the love and devotion we have been called to, *and a way of life.*

If a spiritual lightbulb has not yet gone off in your head, perhaps this will be the final key to get you there. I have not given titles to any of the chapters in this book. I usually don't. But I am giving a title to this chapter. I hope you enjoy.

CHAPTER THIRTEEN

Falling in Love with the Wind

"So don't be surprised when I tell you that you have to be 'born from above' — out of this world, so to speak. You know well enough how the wind blows this way and that. You hear its' rustling through the trees, but you have no idea where it comes from or where it's headed next. <u>That's the way it is with everyone 'born from above' by the wind of God, the Spirit of God.</u>"

— John 3: 7-8 (Message Bible)

By the will of God, we have not married any ordinary fella, but the very Son-of-God, Himself. We have married into a type of godhood, but as Queen, not King. And we have married into a different way of living, called Spirit Life. We are not moved by the ways of this world, but the ways of His world, and His world is symbolized as akin to the wind. It is a life of flow and peace. And usually, our peace within is a good monitor of how we are doing at any given point, as we're learning to walk in the Spirit.

Eagles mount up with mighty wings to soar upon thermal currents, rising currents, in the wind, a picture of Spirit life. The eagle is a bird that flaps less and soars more. When our peace is disturbed it's because we're doing a lot of flapping. We are living in the habit of flapping, not soaring.

There is great power in Spirit life, and only an illusion of power in the flesh. The arm of flesh will fail us, our Bible warns. Think of the freedom of the wind. He who the Son sets free, is free indeed. Jesus greeted people with, "Peace be unto you." The angels declared at His birth, "Peace on earth! Goodwill towards man!" True peace is powerful and leads to true power. The Gospel is also called the Gospel of Peace. Our feet are to be shod with the Gospel of Peace.

Nevertheless, many people, and many Christians will continue living in their flesh, failing to fall in love and fully embrace the ways of our Lord. And what is a good picture of that? I like to answer that question by asking, are you the Captain of a Rowboat, Motorboat, or Sailboat?

These boats are three different ways of life, and only one of them truly knows the power of the Lord. Only one of them is fully in love with the Lord. Only one of them is the Song of Songs. Only one of them can even honestly call Him, "Lord".

God is the Admiral of His Fleet and each of us Captains of our vessel. We are not the Admiral, but we are Captains because we choose how our vessel is going to operate upon the seas of life. We can even choose to ignore the orders of our Admiral. But when we do, be sure to know you have set evil forces against you, and you have greatly weakened God's forces who are for you. Like Jonah thrown over the side of the ship, bad things are coming, even as the story of Hosea and Gomer.

Picture if you will the differences between a Rowboat, or Motorboat, or Sailboat. Two of those boats are powered by man-made ways. One is powered by sheer force of flesh, brute strength and endurance. The other powered by man's intellect. With his brain man designed and invented the combustion engine, the motor, and uses it to power many things.

However, the Sailboat is a very different vessel than the other two, for if the Captain chooses, it can be powered by the wind alone. Not a man-made force, but a force symbolic of Spirit life. Of course, this would require the Captain need know how to be a true sailor. What knowledge does a Sailboat Captain function in, compared to the Captain of a Motorboat or Rowboat? *It is a completely different way of life.*

I picture the Rowboat person as someone very physically oriented. They like working with their hands, perhaps. They prefer physical labor to mental. They will work hard all day swinging a hammer, driving a truck, paving a road, or even an athlete in physical competition. This is the way of life they know and prefer. It is what they have chosen, and they sail the seven seas of life in this way, constantly focused on the physical.

Now the Motorboat Captain might tend to think he is better than everyone else. I'm not saying they are all like that, but loving the ways of "being smart", they look down on living by the sweat of the brow. That's what we invented air conditioning for. Why sweat when you don't have too? I'm smarter than that. Why row a boat when you can invent a motor to do all that work? You can go so much faster! And with less effort! You can even go against the wind if you like! Of course, you do have to have more money, because none of this is free.

I'm sure you've figured out by now that this book is about being the Captain of a Sailboat, and knowing those Sailboat ways, having the knowledge and skills of a true sailor. Can you picture the beauty of a Sailboat gracefully cutting a path across the sea, powered by the wind, sparkling water all around, sails to the full, and an orange glow low on the horizon? Few things cast such a beautiful and peaceful scene. This is beautiful in the sight of our Lord.

True, the Motorboat can make the trip much faster and easier, but at what cost? Not only what cost financially, but also spiritually. My wife grew up water skiing during the summer. As we began dating, I got to do it with her; but I remember the noise of that motor cutting across what that morning had been such a smooth and quiet mirror of nature. A part of me always regretted the effect of the Motorboat on that beautiful lake.

Most Motorboat people lose the quiet soul of the peaceful as they rip and roar in pursuit of their dreams. They become dull of hearing to anything of the Spirit. They are not an Elijah in the cave, or John the Baptist in the wilderness. It's too quiet for them in those places.

When we are first born-again, like any infant, we have much growing ahead of us and it takes time. But as we grow in our walk with the Lord, we might hear Him whispering, "Why don't you cut that motor loose from your Sailboat, and let it drop to the ocean floor? You're a Sailboat now. You don't need that. And while you're at it, throw those oars overboard, too. I think you're ready."

Wow. We might not be ready yet, but the Captain of a Sailboat has that potential. It is there for the taking if they so decide. The other two vessels have no hope of this. If you attach a sail to the Rowboat, it is no longer a Rowboat. It's now a Sailboat. Only a Sailboat has the potential at all times to tap into the Spirit world, Spirit power, and supernatural ways of God. They that wait upon the Lord. The eagle soars more and flaps less as he mounts up with those mighty wings upon the wind.

I hope you see the beauty of what I am describing here. I hope you see the beauty of the book, Song of Songs. I hope you see the beauty of Elijah at the mouth of the cave, John the Baptist in the wilderness, John the Apostle leaning his head on our Lord's shoulder, the beauty of hearing God's whispers and knowing His secrets because He reveals them to those who diligently seek Him. The beauty of our Lord.

We can dwell in the secret place of the Most High and stay under His shadow. In the events I see upon the horizon, indeed, it is the only place to be. It is the reward of those who love the Lord and constantly seek to be with Him. These are the ones who will make the difference when darkness becomes so thick you cannot see where you are going. These ones are not led in earthly ways.

They have another source they have learned to move by. The darkness will not stop them.

When manmade ways begin failing, the Sailboats still have power. When the Motorboat is sputtering from lack of gas, and the Rowboat is too weary to make another stroke, the Sailboat Captain is RESTING in his Lord, sails filled with *heaven's Wind*. This Captain understands a higher way.

In our humanity we love the idea of the Motorboat. The ability to rev the engine and force our way. We want what we want. If I work hard enough, I can be successful. But what is our definition of success? Is it a worldly definition, or Kingdom of God? Is contentment a form of success? Is receiving knowledge from God a form of success? Is not being addicted to material things a form of success?

The Motorboat is not at the mercy of the wind. We love our independence. We love our own will power even when it may be going against that whisper in our ear concerning the will of God. And we don't like to wait. Hear my roar! This is what we like, as we rev that engine and pursue our desires.

Contrary to the Motorboat Captain, I've seen documentaries and movies where a Sailboat Captain might be stuck for hours, possibly even days, with no wind! They are stuck setting there for hours on end! Waiting! Unable to move! Unless temptation causes them to power up the motor. Why not fire up a motor, our logical mind debates. Indeed, why not? Has God really said you will die?

They that wait upon the Lord? Song of Songs is a different way. It is a way of being in love with our Lord and the freedom of the Wind, Spirit Life. By faith we know the Motorboat Captain will eventually find himself in such a storm that his vessel sinks to never be seen again. There is supernatural wisdom in the wind. All Sailboats go to heaven.

You see, it's not just about the type of boat. You've got to also understand the power of the sea. It's about this ocean we're on, too. And the Word of God tells us this ocean is also supernatural. We're not facing just a natural thing here. There is also the unseen world.

There are powers we do not see. Very powerful forces we cannot survive on our own. And somehow, our God has promised us that the Sailboat is the way to go if you want true and eternal success! Those of us who cut the motors loose, we believe Him! And therefore, have attempted to change our life to His ways, *a way in love with the Wind.*

They say God always has His remnant. Do we want to go into the LAST DAYS as part of the herd, or Remnant? There is power in the wind that the Motorboat Captain knows nothing of, but it takes great faith to live that way. This, the Sailboats know. This, the Sailboats greatly desire and seek after. We do not settle for beans and gas. LOL.

There is an incredible illustration of this in God's word that most people miss. We have discussed before how can we know when enough is enough? We have considered how will a people so in love with luxury, ease, entertainment, technology, and pleasure be able to say "NO" to the Mark of the Beast when it comes? It is likely only the Sailboats will have that discernment and power. The Rowboats and Motorboats will need to change or be lost. Let this powerful illustration reveal what I mean.

There are two stories of the Children of Israel asking for meat, or flesh, in the desert. They are desiring flesh. One was blessed of God, and one was not. It's that simple. And the difference is such a great revelation. Every Christian seeking to walk with God should know these two stories by heart. This should be taught in every Church across America over and over again. But if you have not heard it there, you are about to hear it here.

I'm going to approach this different than I usually do. We're going to look at the action of flesh that was NOT blessed, first. And then the blessed way will be so very plain. Here we go… the children of Israel are in their second year of being in the wilderness…

STORY #1

"Now the mixed multitude who were among them yielded to intense craving; so the children of Israel also wept again and said: "Who will give us meat to eat? We remember the fish which we ate freely in Egypt, the cucumbers, the melons, the leeks, the onions, and the garlic; but now our whole being is dried up; there is nothing at all except this manna before our eyes!" — Numbers 11:4-6 (NKJ)

So, we make note here, evidently God expected them to be content with the manna he was providing. Manna only? Realize this is the old covenant time. God expected us to save our self by works. He was actually "revealing to us" that we cannot save our self by works. Our fallen sin nature craves flesh! And we need to realize that. Without God's mercy and grace, we fail every time. We still struggle with this simple lesson.

I believe God's giving them "manna only" was a picture of living in complete holiness. But of course, we cannot. We desire to grow in holiness our whole life, but we never attain "perfection" while still in our flesh. We will always lust for some meat. But how much is enough? Where do we find balance? Where do we draw the line?

Where is contentment? What will God "allow" and "bless", and what will He not? (These two stories when put together are so good!) Let us continue in Story #1.

Jump to verse 31. There is much good material for study in the other verses as well, but for the purposes of this teaching, we take up here...

> "Now a wind went out from the Lord, and it brought quail from the sea and left them fluttering near the camp, about a day's journey on this side and about a day's journey on the other side, all around the camp, and about two cubits above the surface of the ground. And the people stayed up all that day, all night and all the next day, and gathered the quail (he who gathered least gathered ten homers—sixty bushels!); and they spread them out for themselves all around the camp. But while the meat was still between their teeth, before it was chewed, the wrath of the Lord was aroused against the people, and the Lord struck the people with a very great plague. So he called the name of that place Kibroth Hattaavah—(Graves of Gluttony), because there they buried the people who yielded to craving."

Do you see our sin? It will be very plain soon. These people ran all day, all night, and the next day! Our American culture would applaud that! But God does not!

Where is peace? Where is contentment? When is enough enough? Where is trusting God? Faith? Oh that we had such desire for the things of God!

I find it interesting that scriptures note the quail were "fluttering" (flapping?) in the wilderness. God drops us spiritual clues all the time for those who have eyes to see, to notice, learn, change, and be transformed into higher places. (Soar more, flap less.) But how many people never notice, because we are so distracted chasing our desires of the flesh?

These people revved their motors and ran, ran, ran! Sixty bushels was the least collected! They rowed-rowed-rowed unto exhaustion. Story #1 is an illustration of Rowboat and Motorboat ways. The next story illustrates the Sailboat.

Do we live in peace? Do we seek first the Kingdom of God and are satisfied in that? How much do we stress our self out, chasing material things? Do we travel light and easy, or heavy and hard? Is it true, less can be more? Why is this not the main message from our Preachers rather than the typical wealth messages? Have we been preaching gluttony and not even realized it?

STORY #2

This experience takes place in only their second month in wilderness. The other story was two years in.

> "Then the whole congregation of the children of Israel complained against Moses and Aaron in the wilderness. And the children of Israel said to them, "Oh, that we had died by the hand of the Lord in the land of Egypt, when we sat by the pots of meat and when we ate bread to the full! For you have brought us out into this wilderness to kill this whole assembly with hunger." (Notice the two events have basically the very same beginnings, the people complaining and craving meat. No real difference, so far, other than, they have not experienced manna yet. They are likely living on what they carried out of Egypt.)

> "Then the Lord said to Moses, "Behold, I will rain bread from heaven for you. And the people will go out and gather a certain quota every day, that I may test them, whether they will walk in my law or not." — Exodus 16:2

Oh, oh! Notice there is a TEST here. And what is the test? Whether they will obey God or not. Whether they will trust God or not. Whether they will know when enough is enough? Or try to "store up" MORE. What do you think they did? And what do we think we do even today, in our own life? Is this still one of God's main tests? Jesus said, "Consider the birds." (?)

Verse twenty is where we learn that the leftover bread turned to worms and stank. Moses gets very angry at the people for their disobedience. However, it is the meat I really want to get to, for there is a great lesson there.

> *"And the Lord spoke to Moses, saying, 'I have heard the complaints of the children of Israel. Speak to them, saying, At twilight you shall eat meat, and in the morning you shall be filled with bread. And you shall know that I am the Lord your God.'"*
>
> *"So it was that quail came up at evening and covered the camp,"... (Drop mic moment!)*
>
> — Verse 11-13a

Notice the meat was not a day's journey out of the camp, but right "in the camp"! This is an important difference! Ever since I noticed this small detail, and shared it with my wife, we have always considered "what is in the camp" as far as what we desire in life and how hard should we chase it?

We become consumed with chasing MORE and we neglect the spiritual things! We end up with LESS because we major on what should be the minor and minor on what should be the major, i.e. our relationship with God! We should focus on being the Sailboat Captain and not the Motorboat or Rowboat! Learning and living in the ways of *"Sailing", powered by the Wind!*

What will God bless? This is what the eagle knows. God will enable us to live a life of peace and satisfaction, as we soar more and flap less. This is such an important understanding that God led me to as I "considered the birds", as He said in His Sermon on the Mount. I have tried to live by this ever since, and it has been a real blessing.

Jesus said His yoke was easy and His burden light. I spent a lot of years of my early Christian life feeling like I was missing something here, because I was working awfully hard. The keys to God's supernatural are faith, surrender, peace, rest, and obedience. He does the heavy lifting. We need to learn the whole chapter of Psalms 23 in our life. I hope to write a book on that, too. We shall see. *Is it in my camp?*

When it is in the camp, God is allowing it. We can have it and it does not distract or drain us from the Kingdom of God life we should be living. Always ask your soul the question, "Does it appear to be in the camp?" My wife and I ask this often. I hope the vision of living in love with the Wind, as the Captain of a Sailboat, will be an inspiration to you and yours.

As you leave this chapter to enter the last, I hope you see the danger of the LAST DAYS coming and the potential of the Sailboat Captain to sail those waters and not end up a child of the beast, marked with the 666; but a *child of the Wind*, strong and free, empowered of God for eternity, not just a few years of eating beans.

Please let the Holy Spirit of God set this picture in your heart, and brand it upon your brain, your very soul! I have prayed this prayer for myself, and I pray it for you as well. In the Name of Jesus, Amen.

CHAPTER FOURTEEN

A word about END TIMES. All through history, any time there has been a major advancement of some sort, i.e. "progress", it has caused a significant change in culture. We are at such a time again. We are already in it, and the wreckage of the old and new cultures colliding is adding up. Debris lay all around us, and we must adapt or die.

We hear talk of a New World Order. Well, truth is, there have been several new orders come to this planet over the course of history, due to progress causing great change, or perhaps a world war. But this next change coming, due to great advances in technology, has the 666 written all over it. Never before have we actually had the ability to do the things spoken of in Revelation. But now we do. We could literally end up in a movie like the Matrix.

Can we survive in the chaos of change and the debris of the old and new? We probably could, except there are certain things that as the Bride of Christ we are not allowed to do, and we are called to stand against. We are called of the *Wind*, not this world. We sail.

There are many things happening right now that I could point to, but why waste time? Let's go straight to the painfully obvious to anyone who knows their Bible. Let's get to the main event. Our world is going global and digital. We are headed towards a Mark of the Beast at breakneck speed. Do we even realize how close we are?

The progress causing the next big change, this new world order, of course, is anything connected to computers, virtual reality, and Artificial Intelligence (AI). Are these things evil in and of themselves? Of course not. But never before has what was prophesied in Revelation been possible, and now it is. How quickly will they cross the red line? Who's to say? But like shifting a car to the next gear, it can be done as soon as they decide to. The car needs to be accelerated to a certain speed first. Are we there yet? How close are we?

The point is, it is coming. It's no longer a revelation of something in a fantasy world. It is in our reality today. It is the direction everything is going. It won't be stopped. It might be delayed, but it won't be stopped. Too much of the toothpaste is already out of the tube, and an ungodly world neither has the wisdom or the desire to say "no" to any kind of progress. The herd is easily manipulated. Show them an easier way and they will follow.

I've heard they have 3D virtual reality that is so real you can hardly tell it from the real thing. Maybe better than the real thing. How many men will be able to resist the temptation of a different beautiful woman anytime they like? Women they would never be handsome enough to get in reality. How many will decide the real thing is not worth all the work and hassle? Marriage will become less and less? VR will be so much easier.

We are being groomed for this already. All the right words are going out over the air waves, and all the wrong words are being suppressed. All the right things are being promoted as wonderful and good, and all the wrong things are outdated and unenlightened. We have new revelations now. Your old ways are hateful and wrong. You are the problem! You're going to kill granny if you don't take this shot! You evil person!

You may have noticed the word "nationalism" is becoming a bad word. That is because the powers that be want to go International, global. So, the brainwashing has already begun. Now the word "nationalism" has become a "trigger word". Anything it is connected to is automatically bad. It triggers emotions in the brainwashed to react in violent and hateful ways; but you are the hater, not them, because you are the nationalist. That word alone proves you so. Debate over! They cannot think outside the box of their programing. They are fighting an evil nationalist! And when did that become evil? How are they able to do this?

Trigger words. Planted there through a form of brainwashing, psychological attacks to the mind, mental manipulations, they know how to program and manipulate the herd. If you have not fallen prey to the mind control, then it will baffle you why so many people are triggered by certain words and ideas. Ideas that were the accepted norm a short time ago, but now are suddenly taboo!

You won't understand why these people go so crazy over certain words and labels! They use them as weapons! This is psychological warfare of the most-evil kind. Most people today are susceptible to it. They make up the herd. The so-called elite control the media through a love for money and use them to perform the brainwashing of the masses. They can make the masses go whatever direction they want. The elite are in the driver's seat because it is so easy for them to manipulate the herd.

People have become so use to letting other people think for them, they no longer think for themselves. Peer pressure. Political correctness. The fear of not being accepted by the popular, the herd. The fear of being an outcast, or persecuted, the loss of money, fears of attack, the list goes on and on. The fear of being inconvenienced. Losing their beloved lifestyle. So easily manipulated. Fears, fears, and more fears. Claims of being "science", and you're unenlightened and a racist. You don't believe in science? Oh, you're probably one of those Bible thumpers, aren't you.

We, the average people are playing checkers while the elite (very wealthy) are playing chess. They are allowed to play chess not because they are smarter. They are actually stupid, because they think they can force a utopia. Man is not capable of a utopia. This is a proven fact. The nature of man will always rebel against such a thing and ruin it, turn it into a prison, a slavery for the many and luxury for a few.

They are allowed to play chess because they happen to have the money to do so. All poorer people must play checkers. The buy-in for chess is very high. Only the very rich are allowed to play. They're not smarter, their just richer. They love money and have been willing to sell their soul to get it; again, proving them not very smart. Just ask Esau.

They are the ultimate fools for believing we have no supreme designer we will answer to, but all this is just a freak and impossible accident that somehow happened nonetheless. That's the "faith" they live in, while denying the Bible, even while the Bible continues being fulfilled by their own plans every day. How blind is that? How stupid is that? But they know how to manipulate the masses. Fear, fear, fear! Lust, lust, lust.

God predicted everything they are doing. No man can do that. They are the blind leading the blind. It requires more blind faith, or stupidity, to be an unbeliever than to believe in God. It requires more refusal to acknowledge the truth when you look around at all the intricate design in an eyeball, or the human hand, or the sprouting of a seed in dirt, or reproduction, and conclude it's the result of a big bang?! Ignorance gone to seed. Vanity of vanities.

So, in their chess game, they see a one world order. No divisions. All mankind living as one and in harmony. Only problem is, pagan man, man without God, is incapable of doing that. God already saw that plan of man. It led to the days of Noah and a great flood. The book of Genesis already shows us what a united pagan mankind will become.

When man tried to do it again, after the flood and at the Tower of Babel, God confused the languages and divided everyone. Our natural mind logically thinks unity among all mankind is the answer, but we fail to factor in our true nature. It has to become a forced thing, a dictatorship, and sooner or later an evil dictator comes to power and what was meant for good becomes horribly bad!

They think they are so smart, but they are short-sighted and stupid. They reject the wisdom of God's Word even though it is proven over and over again. They persist in forcing a world order that scripture shows can only fail. They think they are better than us and know what is best, but I can make my own decisions, thank-you. I have my own brainwashing, thank you. I have washed my mind in the Word of God over and over again. I know how to find my way through your darkness.

But they are the Motorboats of the world, forcing their will on the masses, on the herd. We are nothing but cows to them. Or perhaps they see us as Rowboats. But they cannot achieve their goals without the power to do so. So, they are making all their moves on the chessboard, wheeling and dealing, making strategic alignments and agreements in the hope of having enough power to rev their man-made Motorboat and force their will.

The book of Revelation says they will be given seven years of success. Success as defined by them. But as we already know, it will all turn terribly bad. Unfortunately, many will die and be executed before the truth is finally known. The progress that will eventually come is one we cannot partake in. How will we suddenly say "NO" to something we've been saying "YES" to our whole life? How will we say "NO" to more comfort, more fun, more convenience, more luxury, and more pleasure? Even the survival of our life? That is the real question, isn't it? Will we even have the eyes to see?

Our country is already under a controlled demolition, an intentional sabotage. We could save it. We could turn it around. But our culture of pleasure seekers are never going to say "no" to the newest toys coming out in the name of fun, pleasure, ease, and progress. So, we are doomed. It's already set. The only question is, how soon? How quickly? And will you take the mark? Or slowly starve? Become homeless. End up in a camp and executed. Wow... and we thought Ecclesiastes was depressing!

Another nail in the coffin to America is that our forefathers already warned us our Constitution would fail in an ungodly culture. It is unworkable! The enemy knows this! They warned us that as soon as the average American realized they could vote themselves money and benefits, they would, and this would be the beginning of the end. Our greedy society, many Christians included, has put this nation into such horrendous "debt" as they cry for their lustful desires of ease and wealth. Our own personal gain more important than what might be the better way. More important than the welfare of the whole. Who cares what it does to them, as long as I get mine? Who cares about the big picture? I'm focused on my little world of me, my, and mine.

This is very "ugly" in the sight of God! Consider these verses from our Lord:

> *"How can I account for this generation? The people have been like spoiled children whining to their parents. We wanted to skip rope, and you were always too tired; we wanted to talk, but you were always too busy. John came fasting and they called him crazy. I came feasting and they called me a boozer, a friend of misfits."*
>
> — Matthew 11, starting verse 16
> (Message Bible)

Spoiled children. We wanted…we wanted… And no matter what God did, they called it evil. He could give them the opposite of a thing, and neither was good, all was evil no matter what, because they had their own ungodly agenda and could not allow John the Baptist or Jesus the Christ to take the power from them. Let the whole world go to hell, but we will maintain our positions of power for however long we can. There is nothing new under the sun. Man's nature, without Christ, remains the same.

The true Bride of the Lamb will shine bright in this time. There will be some Elijahs in this time also, but many will be called upon to be a martyr. If you are, take heart, you're in the greatest of company. Men like John the Baptist, the Apostles, and even Jesus Himself, and many others all down through history. Martyrs have a habit of overcoming death, so take heart. And do not trade your spiritual birthright for a temporary pot of beans like Esau did. God hated Esau; but loved Jacob. As the Bride, we are Jacob, who becomes Israel, *one who has power with God, Champion of God!*

It's so sad that it all comes to this. And why would I, in a book of this topic, the Bride of the Lamb, bring up such a horrendous ending? Because we are the problem. We left our first love. Look around, it is so obvious to see. This is coming because all us Christians who have played the harlot.

We rejected Song of Songs to be Gomer in the book of Hosea. So, I'm asking each of us to repent now! Get back to our first love and back to being the Shulamite! While we still can! Don't waste any time! We've got to make this effort, this surrender. Because if God raises up any Elijahs in this time, they will be firebrands from out of His Bride! I would be remiss if I did not point out our calling as the Bride of the Lamb in these end times.

God gave us the game plan and it never changes, no matter what. The elite can play chess all they want, but God's checkers will beat pagan chess any day. Jesus told us to love. To love God with all our heart and love others as our self. Is that simple enough? And if we do this, we are the Bride, and we are highly trained in spiritual warfare, not to fight against flesh and blood, but the real principalities hiding behind it all.

The Elijahs of the world understand the simplicity of Christ. They understand the simplicity of what Christ started. Again, I ask, how long do you think your big Church buildings are going to be able to function when all these hate-speech laws come into full effect in the new order? I suspect our ranks will be severely reduced before we even get to the Mark of the Beast. Either a Church will compromise their message in order to keep the doors open, or go to jail. A true Church will not compromise.

I have said for years now, we should disconnect from the government tax break given to the Church. Why are we beholden to them? This is only another strangle hold they have on our modern Church. How do we not see the things that are so plainly in sight? Where is our vision distracted to? For there are no other explanations of how God's people could be so foolish and blind.

I would dare to say, any Church not already establishing a strong small groups ministry meeting in homes and such, is not hearing God. They are living in denial of what is coming. They are in love with their fancy and high-cost building and going to be caught with their pants down. It will be very embarrassing, but well-deserved. Prayer of Elijah.

We talked about hearing God's whispers. Those who hear God's whispers have been hearing this for a long time. It's not even a whisper anymore. I believe God is shouting! And still, half the Church does not hear.

Rise up Shulamites! Rise up from your cozy bed! We may already be too late. We got to the door to late. Our Lord has left and the bitterness of myrrh is on our hands! But the true Shulamites will go out into the night searching for her Lover! She will be beaten and suffer hard things! But in the end, she will find her Lord in His garden, in His high mountains of spices, and they will be together forever.

His Name, and His Ring.

THE BEGINNING… Go forth and multiply.

"Because he has set his love upon me, I will deliver him. <u>I will set him on high, because he has known my name."</u>

— Psalms 91 (KJV)

ABOUT THE AUTHOR"

My Bible College has been many Churches, Pastors, Evangelists, Camps, Spiritual Retreats, preached messages, books read, and study of my Bible for sixty-eight years. I was raised in Church from a baby, and I cannot begin to estimate how much teaching I have heard, messages preached, and books read over these many years.

Secondly, I have had a love for God and the Bible my whole life, and therefore have spent countless hours in the quiet places, asking God questions, trying to hear His answers, and studying His book. I'm always seeking more of His Holy Spirit, because I believe more of His Holy Spirit is the real answer to every question we have and every difficulty we face.

I married a lovely young lady when I was twenty-one. We have been married forty-eight years, raised five children and have eleven grandchildren. We have done everything from many years of youth ministry, to also preaching and teaching to adults, teaching in small home groups which I love, and even served as a Church janitor cleaning toilets. My Church experience is wide ranging.

These are some of the "good things" that might qualify me to write such a book worth people's precious time to read. But never forget, I am a mortal human being just like you, still wrapped in flesh, and always asking God to work on my own personal flaws. I'm an imperfect man trying to share a perfect Christ.

I pray this little book go forth to help and inspire as many people as God might enable, and that my own shortcomings do not get in the way. *"Bless the Lord oh my soul; and forget none of HIS benefits."* Amen.

Please send comments and requests to the author:
jonahjoe2025@gmail.com

Made in the USA
Columbia, SC
31 January 2025

52503131R00091